PRAISE FOR THE

'Jonathan has written the book which sums up the work he leads in Canterbury Diocese. It is deeply based in the Bible, centred on people made in the image of God and founded on the love and authority of Jesus Christ. It is accessible to read and challenging to think about, vivid about people and rubs at our rough edges of selfishness, visionary in application and practical in use. It is a great gift to the church that brings together talking and showing the gospel.'
Justin Welby, Archbishop of Canterbury

'Jonathan's theologically rich yet accessible consideration of the practice of doing justice through the rhythms, tunes and modes of music opens up a fresh vista. This fired my imagination. I heard beautiful and intriguing things. Here is the sort of "new song" that we need to hear in an ever-needy world.'
Very Revd Dr David Monteith, dean of Canterbury

'*The Everyday God* is a must read, in which Jonathan Arnold offers the challenge that the church, and every Christian, needs to be reminded of over and over again: that the kingdom of God, seen in the person of Jesus Christ, is one of justice and mercy, which is care for all people and all creation. This is an inspiring and useful book for individuals of all ages, for small groups, or whole congregations, in which you cannot help but be moved in heart, mind and to action as Dr Arnold encourages us that "at our best, as human beings, we begin to join the symphony and the dance of the divine Trinity of God."'
Very Revd Jo Kelly-Moore, dean of St Albans

'The cry for justice is a common and oft-repeated theme in the scriptures. Jonathan Arnold, priest, singer and director of the Social Justice Network, has a unique view of the interwoven themes that are given voice in this book. In theological and musical reflection on action that is grounded in the reality of the world and human need, our understanding of God's love for the world is deepened. We still need both to sing the songs of God's justice and to hear the cry of those who seek it.'
Venerable Dr Will Adam, archdeacon of Canterbury

'*The Everyday God* is a ringing affirmation of faith in God's justice and mercy and how it transforms our everyday attitudes and actions.'
Canon Angela Tilby, canon emerita of Christ Church Cathedral, Oxford, writer and broadcaster

THE EVERYDAY GOD

ENCOUNTERING THE DIVINE
IN THE WORKS OF MERCY

JONATHAN ARNOLD

BRF
Ministries

 Ministries

15 The Chambers, Vineyard
Abingdon OX14 3FE
+44 (0)1865 319700 | brf.org.uk

Bible Reading Fellowship (BRF) is a charity (233280)
and company limited by guarantee (301324),
registered in England and Wales

ISBN 978 1 80039 210 6
First published 2024
10 9 8 7 6 5 4 3 2 1 0
All rights reserved

Text © Jonathan Arnold 2024
This edition © Bible Reading Fellowship 2024
Cover photos: sandwiches (left) and mother and child (centre) © Kirrilee Reid; all other photos
from Pixabay (Erika Wittlieb, imsogabriel, niekverlaan), Unsplash (Christian Lue, Nathan
Dumlao), BRF Ministries. Author photo © Chris Henry Photography
Interior photos: colour plates (see p. 8 for details) © Ghislaine Howard; pen-on-paper sketch
and notes (pp. 200–01) © Andrew Feltham

The author asserts the moral right to be identified as the author of this work

Acknowledgements

Unless otherwise acknowledged, scripture quotations are taken from the New Revised
Standard Version Updated Edition. Copyright © 2021 National Council of Churches of Christ
in the United States of America. Used by permission. All rights reserved worldwide. Scripture
quotations marked with the following abbreviations are taken from the version shown: **ESV**:
The Holy Bible, English Standard Version, Anglicised edition, published by HarperCollins
Publishers, © 2001 Crossway Bibles, a division of Good News Publishers. Used by permission.
All rights reserved. **NKJV**: the New King James Version®. Copyright © 1982 by Thomas Nelson.
Used by permission. All rights reserved. **NIV**: the Holy Bible, New International Version®
Anglicised, NIV® Copyright © 1979, 1984, 2011 by Biblica, Inc.® Used by permission. All rights
reserved worldwide. **KJV**: The Authorised Version of the Bible (The King James Bible), the
rights in which are vested in the Crown, reproduced by permission of the Crown's Patentee,
Cambridge University Press. **NAB**: the New American Bible, revised edition © 2010, 1991, 1986,
1970 Confraternity of Christian Doctrine, Inc., Washington, DC All Rights Reserved.

'The Come-as-you-are Ceilidh' from *Melodies of New Monasticism*, by Craig Gardner (pp. 56–57)
is © Craig Gardiner, 2018, published in the United Kingdom by SCM Press. Used by permission.
rights@hymnsam.co.uk

Every effort has been made to trace and contact copyright owners for material used in
this resource. We apologise for any inadvertent omissions or errors, and would ask those
concerned to contact us so that full acknowledgement can be made in the future.

A catalogue record for this book is available from the British Library

Printed and bound by CPI Group (UK) Ltd, Croydon CR0 4YY

For Emma, with love

CONTENTS

LIST OF PLATES

About the artist

Ghislaine Howard (1953–) first came to public attention with her ground-breaking exhibition concerning pregnancy and birth, 'A Shared Experience' in 1993, which was shown at Manchester Art Gallery and the Wellcome Foundation, London.

Her large cycle of paintings The Stations of the Cross / The Captive Figure was created in association with Amnesty International in 2000. The 14 monumental works were exhibited to great acclaim at the two Liverpool Cathedrals and have since toured cathedrals throughout the UK. She was named as a 'Woman of The Year' in 2008 for her contribution to art and society.

In 2013 her *Pregnant Self-Portrait*, 1987 was the centre piece of the British Museum's exhibition, 'Ice-Age Art: The arrival of the modern mind'. She has featured in various publications and television documentaries, including Mischa Scorer's multi-award winning *Degas and The Dance*, and her work may be found in many public and private collections, including The Royal Collection.

She is currently working on a ten-year project, 10 Boroughs / 10 Paintings, in collaboration with the city of Manchester and the Greater Manchester Chamber of Commerce.

Works of Mercy

In 2010, Ghislaine saw two small medieval paintings in Madrid relating to the seven acts of mercy. So began a commitment to work towards producing seven large ambitious oil paintings on that theme. Though Christian in origin, the seven acts represent values that are found at the heart of all the world's major religions and form the basis of any decent, civilised community. They are: feed the hungry; visit the sick; give drink to the thirsty; clothe the naked; shelter the homeless; visit the imprisoned and bury the dead.

More information about Ghislaine may be found at **ghislainehoward. com** and in *Ghislaine Howard, the Human Touch: Paintings, drawings and prints, 1980–2016*, written by her husband, the art historian, Michael Howard.

A NOTE ON REFERENCES TO GOD

References to God have been made gender neutral as much as possible in this book. However, it has not been possible to avoid pronouns completely and, in accordance with the publisher's conventions, a masculine pronoun has been used in cases where a pronoun has been needed.

FOREWORD

■ ■

'What does the Lord require of us? To act justly, to love mercy and to walk humbly with our God' (Micah 6:8) These are words from the prophet Micah penned in the eighth century BCE and yet still relevant today. I am grateful to Jonathan Arnold for reminding us of the need for justice and mercy to be at the heart of who we are and all that we do as the people of God. The final prayer said by the whole church at the end of the Eucharist includes these words: 'Send us out in the power of the Spirit, to live and work to your praise and glory.' This is our collective commitment to go out and be the hands, feet and voice of Jesus to those most vulnerable in our communities and in our world. This is not an optional extra that we do if we feel like it.

As I have travelled in different parts of the Anglican Communion, I have seen first hand the church, present and engaged in the lives of ordinary people, providing health care, education, food and shelter, care facilities for orphans, the elderly and the abused. Here in the diocese of Canterbury, Jonathan is uniquely placed in his leadership of The Social Justice Network to help the wider church reflect on the presence of the everyday God in the work being done with refugees and asylum seekers, the variety of programmes to feed the hungry across the diocese, creating homes for those leaving the prison system and all the time enabling the church to make the connection between faith and works. As church we are called to speak truth to power, to hold to account those who seek to lead politically, pointing them always towards justice and mercy.

The Everyday God encourages us to see the works of mercy in Matthew 25:34–40 as a call to prayer in action and encounter with the divine. When we feed the hungry, give drink to the thirsty, shelter the homeless, visit the prisoner and welcome the stranger, we are encountering Christ himself. We are transformed by our encounter with Christ, but we do not stop there, we become conduits for others. Canterbury diocese casts the vision of 'Changed Lives – Changing Lives'. As our lives are changed by our encounter with Christ, we become enablers for others to have their lives transformed too, and they in turn become instruments of change for others.

The application of *The Everyday God* can be used by individuals and groups. I am personally excited to have this accessible book for local parishes to engage with. It creates the possibility for local groups to ask the question that Micah asked, 'What does the Lord require of us?' The answer each church arrives at will vary according to the context they are in, but there will be a common thread: mercy and justice must be an expression of all the work we do. This timely and important book is a prophetic call for all, and I hope you are inspired, energised, moved and encouraged in your faith and action.

As Jesus lay in his mother's womb, Mary sang her song of praise echoing God's justice and his mercy. May that be our song and our work daily as we walk with *The Everyday God*.

Rt Revd Rose Hudson-Wilkin
Bishop of Dover

PRELUDE

In many ways this book is a product of the Covid-19 pandemic. A few months before lockdown I had taken up a position directing a diocesan department engaged with community outreach, social justice and environmental action, working with refugees, the homeless and the marginalised in south-east England and northern France. As you can imagine, lockdown had a profound effect upon community groups and projects of all kinds. Community meals and hubs were temporarily closed, food banks had to change their way of working, meetings went online and our streets went quiet.

One noticeable consequence of staying home was the reduction in sound. Not only in our streets but also in our skies. Without the noise of traffic and aeroplanes we could hear birds again in our cities, but inside our public buildings, where voices had rung out, now there was only hush. Our theatres, lecture halls, churches, shops and cafés were transformed into empty spaces. If we wanted to speak or listen to another human being, it would often be through the medium of a computer or a phone.

But what I most missed in terms of public interaction was enjoying, sharing in and participating in live music. Before ordination I had been a professional singer and had never imagined there would come a time when every church, concert hall and cathedral would be silent. It was not just the inability to hear live music that particularly affected me, but also the lack of opportunities to sing with other people – to engage in the embodied, physiological, psychological, emotional and spiritual act of singing in community, together. As the months progressed this prohibition had a lasting imprint on my psyche, and that of many others. I would never take communal singing, or any other communal activity, for granted again.

So, as we emerged out of confinement for the last time and our community groups began to open their doors again, certain priorities emerged or evolved. We could sing again. My department, or 'framework', in the diocese took time to rethink its aims and objectives and, after much debate, facilitation and discussion, emerged as the Social Justice Network charity. The seeds of this book were sown, as together our team reflected personally and theologically on what we had been through, and where we were going.

> **Music is an apt metaphor to use to describe how we are to live in Christian community.**

This is all to explain, or perhaps justify, the tone of this work. As music and other communal activities have emerged again, the temptation to think about community in musical terms has been a strong one. And the more reflecting I have done, the more it seems to me that music is an apt metaphor to use to describe how we are to live in Christian community, and how we are to relate to God and to one another. St Augustine once wrote: 'God is music.' What did he mean? I hope that in the following exploration we may find, together, at least some ways in which this might be true.

Jonathan Arnold.

OVERTURE

■ ■

> If you read the Bible, if you look at it at all, constantly [God] was showing up in people's lives at the worst possible time of their life.

Mike Yaconelli

> 'For I was hungry and you gave me food, I was thirsty and you gave me drink, I was a stranger and you welcomed me, I was naked and you clothed me, I was sick and you visited me, I was in prison and you came to me... Truly, I say to you, as you did it to one of the least of these my brothers, you did it to me.'

MATTHEW 25:35–36, 40 (ESV)

Everything that follows is based upon a belief that God is active in our everyday lives. This belief is in turn based upon two premises: first, the evidence of the life, teaching, ministry, death and resurrection of Jesus Christ as presented in the Bible; and second, personal experience of a lived reality with God in the everyday through knowledge of Christ and grace of the Holy Spirit. You may or may not share this belief, or even be curious about it. But the fact that you are reading this suggests you might be. You may think that there is enough evil and suffering in the world to demonstrate that God is nowhere to be seen or heard in our pain. But this book argues that it is precisely here where God is to be found: in our pain, our loss, our suffering; also in our joy, hope, anxiety, boredom, loneliness, drudgery or contentment, in the everyday. More specifically, the evidence of Christ's humble and sacrificial life of service, teaching and healing suggests that he most especially identifies with the poor, the oppressed and the suffering.

If what I believe is true – that the 'Christ event' of 2,000 years ago was the self-emptying and self-disclosure of God by entering the depths of our humanity to bring salvation and life – then we cannot ignore it, because with that belief comes a response to a call. The call comes *from* love and is a call *to* love. This book is an exploration of how we can hear, and tune into, the sweet music of that call, and how we might join in with Christ's music of mercy, justice and love.

To love God with all our being, to love ourselves and to love our neighbour is a lifelong endeavour and adventure. To explore how we can connect with, participate in and be 'in tune' with the divine action of God in the world, I am going to draw some help from the vocabulary of music. Concepts and images from the musical world will form a metaphorical backdrop to our theological reflection. For, as the poet Gerard Manley Hopkins wrote: 'Christ plays in ten thousand places, in lovely limbs and eyes not his.'

The music of mercy and justice – Christ plays in ten thousand places

> *Í say móre: the just man justices;*
> *Keeps grace: thát keeps all his goings graces;*
> *Acts in God's eye what in God's eye he is –*
> *Chríst – for Christ plays in ten thousand places,*
> *Lovely in limbs, and lovely in eyes not his*
> *To the Father through the features of men's faces.*
> Gerard Manley Hopkins, 'As kingfishers catch fire'

These words speak of the acceptance of God's grace, and how grace can transform our everyday behaviour and actions, allowing a person to be 'in God's eye what in God's eye he is' – that is, a bearer of Christ. Christ plays in ten thousand places, in our limbs, our eyes, and God can be perceived in the faces of others. Manley Hopkins knew that Christ is everywhere. Christ is the unbegotten foundation of creation, for 'without him nothing was made that was made' (John 1:3,

NK JV), and Christ is incarnated everywhere, in human bodies, minds and expressions and in creation. Christ as God and fully human is therefore everywhere and in the everyday, not remote or invisible. As a consequence, not only can we see Christ at work in the world every day through his actions of justice, kindness and mercy, but we can also perceive him in the 'lovely in limbs and eyes not his'.

The theological paradox that is at play here has its basis in Matthew 25, where Christ, at one and the same time, calls us to be involved in his works of mercy, but also equips us through his grace so that God may work in and through us to make his actions possible. It is both a command and a gift, creating moments when God is manifest 'in ten thousand places', in everyday people, places and things; when we see, feel and know Christ in the personal, the individual, in the natural world, in the now, whether through transformation, peace, comfort or his energising power.

In his interpretation of Manley Hopkins' poem, Craig Gardiner extends the visual element to the aural, or sonic, by using the musical metaphor of 'polyphony', which literally means 'many voices or sounds'. Polyphony is a term used to describe music with interweaving tunes or melodies that are different yet complementary, overlapping and yet harmonious. In many ways community can be described in terms of polyphony: 'The many melodies of this Christ are revealed in the faces and lives of numerous people… whose very being is an act of worship to the Father',[1] just as Manley Hopkins's poem weaves themes of humanity and divinity together, connected by the melodious interaction of justice, grace, limbs, eyes and faces, Father and Son. In this sense, the phrase 'in God's eye what in God's eye he is' could be 'transposed from a visual to an aural metaphor: to be in God's ear the melody that God already hears for us. The purpose of humanity is to play out these melodies that God hears in the reality of the world'.[2] In this way, Manley Hopkins' ideas reflect those of Old Testament prophets, such as Isaiah, where actions of justice and kindness, rather than malice and spite, are perceived as the true way in which all are called to reflect the divine image.

> If you remove the yoke from among you,
>> the pointing of the finger, the speaking of evil,
> if you offer your food to the hungry
>> and satisfy the needs of the afflicted,
> then your light shall rise in the darkness
>> and your gloom be like the noonday.
>
> ISAIAH 58:9–10

It is for this reason that the structure of this book is based around the seven works of mercy, those practical and down-to-earth acts that can reflect God's grace in the world.

The everyday God

To talk about an everyday God is to recognise that to live fully as a Christian is to see and hear where God is acting, whether inside or outside our churches, and to join in with that work. The music of our mission as Christians is to join in with the melody of the *missio Dei*, God's mission.

I am fortunate to work with a team of skilled and passionate people who manage projects aligned with the seven works of mercy. The Social Justice Network team is an outward-facing framework of the diocese that works to express our faith in God through work in high-profile topical issue areas, such as prisons, homelessness, deprivation and forced migration. We build relationships with partner networks to discern and develop new audiences for future engagement.

Every day there are stories of healing and hope. Every day there are stories of healing and hope. This book has emerged as a testament to these initiatives and in response to the many social and community projects within our parishes, villages and towns. Drawing upon this experience in community, I hope to explore how the biblical imperative to love one's neighbour through practical and applied faith is evident in the works of mercy found in Matthew 25:35–40 and in people today, and how these works of mercy are a means of grace, through which God gives blessing, forgiveness, life and salvation.

Through these true stories of everyday lives lived courageously and generously in the service of one another, *The Everyday God* shares observations of lives transformed through the dedication of ordinary people seeking to follow Christ, and thereby reflects upon Jesus' call to feed the hungry, clothe the naked (shelter the homeless), give drink to the thirsty, heal the sick, visit the imprisoned, welcome the stranger and bury the dead. Pope Francis added an extra spiritual work of mercy in 2016, to care for our environment, which will also be explored in this work.

By using the term 'everyday God', I am not referring to the idea that 'God is not just for Sunday', '24/7 discipleship' or 'fresh expressions' of being church, nor am I centred on who we are and what we do as Christians, but rather on *who* God is, *where* God is and *what* God is doing there. It is God's music, Christ's melody that is playing, and if we tune in and listen, we might be able to hear it, be moved by it, sing along with it. We might even find ourselves in harmony with it and with one another.

If there is an 'everyday God', then I guess there must also be an 'everyday theology', which you and I are now engaged in. So, what is it? Kevin Vanhoozer describes everyday theology as 'faith seeking understanding of everyday life. Nothing should be easier to understand than the notion of "the everyday" for the simple reason that it is so commonplace.'[3] It is therefore a curiosity, a seeking, a questioning born out of our faith. And hence we don't need any special place or institution to be an everyday theologian. Our research laboratory is the everyday and the ordinary, whatever and wherever that might be for you, because God's grace is in the everyday.

God is revealed through the ordinary, because God is at the very heart of every human experience. Through the creation of the world, through the Logos (Christ), to the incarnation of Jesus, God has demonstrated that he dwells with us, as Paul Tillich put it, 'as the ground of our being'.[4] This divine gift of grace at the depths of our human existence is Christ's identification with 'the least' (Matthew 25:40).

We do not, therefore, treat our neighbour as a means to an end, a means to receiving or invoking divine grace. Rather, we see that the everyday encounter is made holy. It follows that we love and serve our neighbour for their own sake, as they do for us, and in so doing forget our own selfish concerns. Only then can the encounter be grace-filled. The challenge that God's work in the world sets for us is how to tune into God's love, service, mercy and justice. How do we connect with the work of God? How do we join in with the music of God and play his theme of mercy.

The works of mercy

The works of mercy mentioned by Christ in Matthew 25 are known as 'corporal', because they pertain to the body, or *corpus*, and are about our physical needs. The six works of mercy named by Jesus are to feed the hungry, give drink to the thirsty, to clothe the naked, to welcome the stranger, to visit the prisoner and to visit the sick. The seventh work of mercy, to bury the dead, is not mentioned in Matthew 25 but comes from the book of Tobit and was added to the list later in Christian history. The importance of performing these duties was urged on Christians from the earliest days of the church, in fact from Christ's declaration of the two highest commandments:

> He said to him, '"You shall love the Lord your God with all your heart and with all your soul and with all your mind." This is the greatest and first commandment. And a second is like it: "You shall love your neighbour as yourself." On these two command-ments hang all the Law and the Prophets.
> MATTHEW 22:37–40

Fulfilling the works of mercy therefore goes hand in hand with loving God and our neighbour. As St John of the Cross wrote: 'At the evening of life, we shall be judged on our love.' For Aquinas, the virtue of practising mercy was part of the greater command and virtue of love, and for him it was this virtue which was the essence of the divine.[5]

In Catholic theology, the seven works of corporal mercy were complemented by the seven spiritual works of mercy, whose purpose was to relieve spiritual suffering. These are: to instruct the ignorant; to counsel the doubtful; to admonish sinners; to comfort the afflicted; to bear wrongs patiently; to forgive offences willingly; and to pray for the living and the dead.

Of course, this passage from Matthew's gospel has caused theological debate throughout history, insisting as it does that according to our merciful deeds, or lack of them, we shall be judged and sentenced to everlasting heaven or hell. In Catholic theology, this seeming endorsement of justification by works stands against the view that God's grace is offered to us freely in the sacraments. In Protestant theology, Jesus' words seem to contrast with the Lutheran imperative that we are justified to God by faith alone.

Such debates will no doubt remain as we struggle to understand the nature of creation and our place within it, but what can unify theological or religious difference is the fundamental sense that all of us are made by a merciful God and in God's image, and our purpose is to worship and love that creator and to exercise love towards each other as we are best able to do. This involves treating others, especially those with whom we strongly disagree or whom we dislike, as holy, uniquely loved children of God. We are commanded to treat the stranger as if they were Christ by offering what we can to help or comfort and in this way to join in with God's grace, which is at work in this world, singing the song of mercy and justice.

It is important to note at this stage that the efficacy of the works of mercy is grounded on God's mercy and not our own. St Bernard of

Clairvaux asked: 'What can I count on? My own merits? No. My merit is God's mercy… If the mercies of the Lord are manifold, I too will abound in merits.'[6]

Moreover, these works of mercy are not just about satisfying people's material needs – of food, drink, shelter and so on. It is not just about the alleviation of material poverty. It is much deeper than that; it is also about prayer, sacrifice and love, as Mother Teresa said:

> If we pick up a man hungry for bread, we give him bread and we have satisfied his hunger. But if we meet a man who is terribly lonely, rejected, discarded by society… material assistance will not help him. For to eliminate that loneliness, to eliminate that terrible pain, he needs prayer, he needs sacrifice, he needs tenderness and love.[7]

For it is by loving the other that one becomes a true disciple of Jesus and that the face of the Father is revealed. God's commandment to love one's neighbour is a single and coherent rule of life. It is for this reason that a Year of Mercy in the Roman Catholic Church was declared in 2016, to promote compassion and combat disrespect and discrimination.

An everyday God

By way of introduction, we begin with an exploration of how God can be found at the very depths of our human experience, how Christ's song of mercy and justice, which is so clearly expressed in the Bible, is the 'musical' thread that runs through the fabric of our world. We will explore how our world, in its fervent individualism, has become out of tune with God and with one another. There is dissonant and cacophonous noise in a society where the voices of the rich drown out the melodies of the marginalised, where the power of privilege ignores the plight of the poor.

We will then explore the word 'mercy' and outline some definitions and parameters for our use of the word 'justice'. Thereafter we examine where the church, as the body of Christ, has lived out its mandate to be merciful and just in the recent past and where we might be now. We will also explore our blind spots, such as the problems and restrictions of (white, male, western, colonial) privilege, question how we can talk about these issues with any integrity, and reflect upon recent theological writings around poverty, privilege, 'being with' and 'being interrupted'.

A book of stories

In the summer of 2023, the Social Justice Network collaborated with Canterbury Cathedral in a series of public lectures on the works of mercy. Revd Dr Emma Pennington, the canon missioner, invited expert speakers in the field of social justice from the network and other partnerships to come and give short talks, and answer questions about their work, life and ministry, in order to share ideas and practice. The lectures built upon the Cathedral's Benedictine monastic heritage. When St Benedict established his rule of life in the early sixth century, he declared that he was establishing a 'school of the Lord's service'. He instructed his monks to receive all guests as Christ, 'for he will say, "I was a stranger and you welcomed me"'.[8] In chapter 36 of his rule, he wrote that the 'care of the sick must rank above and before all else so that they may truly be served as Christ', being patiently borne with and suffering no neglect.[9] And again in chapter 4: 'You must relieve the lot of the poor, clothe the naked, visit the sick (Matthew 25:36), and bury the dead. Go to help the troubled and console the sorrowing. Your way of acting should be different from the world's way; the love of Christ must come before all else.'[10]

Therefore, the substance of this book includes wisdom from each of the lectures given, as well as first-hand interview material from those working to show God's mercy and bring justice and love to the world. Each chapter on the works of mercy (chapters 4–11) will begin with some Bible passages relating to the theme of the chapter, including (for chapters 4–9) the relevant text from Matthew 25:35–36. Theological reflection on stories and testimonies will follow in each chapter, with human encounter at the heart of these tales of transformation and hope. Each chapter will end with a spiritual, scriptural exercise, some suggestions for further thought and reading, and links to useful websites or resources.

Conclusion

The everyday God is visible through works and actions every day, and is a God who is for everyone, rich or poor, privileged or lowly, addicted or clean, intellectual or uneducated. The everyday God appears in ordinary events and people and often is manifest in the most unexpected or seemingly unlikely places.

God calls us to move out of our comfort zones and into his liminal space on the margins of our society, to see the face of Christ in a stranger, whose language and culture we may not know, and who yet brings us grace and blessings from afar. We may also see the everyday God in the progress of a young man released from prison who is given dignity, trust, respect, and the chance of a home and a life away from addiction and crime. We can feel the everyday God in the joy and freedom of singing together old familiar songs and laughing in friendship with those living with dementia. And we see the everyday God in a refugee who, having fled persecution, has no home, as Jesus himself once experienced.

I hope this book encourages you to look for God in the everyday, in every circumstance and in every person. For Christ plays in ten thousand places, in our limbs, our eyes and our ears, and through his grace he works mercy every day.

A prayer as we journey through this book together

Dear Lord, we praise you for your creative and sustaining love. We thank you that each one of us, your children, is uniquely precious to you, our maker and redeemer. As we seek to live your kingdom values every day, we pray that your Holy Spirit may give us the wisdom, courage and strength to shelter the homeless, welcome the stranger, visit the prisoner and the sick, clothe the naked, give food to the hungry and drink to the thirsty, and care for the dying and give them dignity at their days' end. Be with us this and every day, and inspire our hearts, we pray, with your flame of love. Through Jesus Christ our Lord. Amen.

Further reading

Gustavo Gutiérrez, *A Theology of Liberation: History, politics, and salvation*, trans. Sister Caridad Inda and John Eagleson (Orbis, 1988).

Saint Bernard Abbot of Clairvaux: Selections from his writings, trans. Horatio Grimley (Cambridge University Press, 2013).

Mother Teresa, Nobel Peace prize speech, 1979, **nobelprize.org/ prizes/peace/1979/teresa/acceptance-speech**

1

THE MELODY OF MERCY

One cannot understand a true Christian who is not merciful, just as one cannot comprehend God without his mercy. This is the epitomizing word of the Gospel: mercy. It is the fundamental feature of the face of Christ.

Pope Francis[11]

Humanity is in eternal discord, in schism, in ceaseless argument with itself. And its inner path is, on the one hand, determined by its own laws, by inexpressible inner events, by changes in the mysterious landscapes of its soul, and, on the other hand, is dependent on the inner path of the epoch in which we live, reflect, collaborate with it.

Mother Maria Skobtsova[12]

Then Jesus said, 'There was a man who had two sons. The younger of them said to his father, "Father, give me the share of the wealth that will belong to me." So he divided his assets between them. A few days later the younger son gathered all he had and travelled to a distant region, and there he squandered his wealth in dissolute living. When he had spent everything, a severe famine took place throughout that region, and he began to be in need. So he went and hired himself out to one of the citizens of that region, who sent him to his fields to feed the pigs. He would gladly have filled himself with the pods that the pigs were eating, and no one gave him anything. But when he came to his senses he said, "How many of my father's hired hands have bread enough and to spare, but here I am dying of hunger! I will get up and go to my father, and I will say to him, 'Father, I have sinned against heaven and before you; I am no longer worthy to be called your son; treat me like one of your hired hands.'" So he set off and went to his father. But while he was still far off, his father saw him and was filled with compassion; he ran and put his arms around him and kissed him. Then the son said to him, "Father, I have sinned against heaven and before you; I am no longer worthy to be called your son." But the father said to his slaves, "Quickly, bring out a robe – the best one – and put it on him; put a ring on his finger and sandals on his feet. And get the fatted calf and kill it, and let us eat and celebrate, for this son of mine was dead and is alive again; he was lost and is found!" And they began to celebrate.

'Now his elder son was in the field, and as he came and approached the house, he heard music and dancing. He called one of the slaves and asked what was going on. He replied, "Your brother has come, and your father has killed the fatted calf, because he has got him back safe and sound." Then he became angry and refused to go in. His father came out and began to plead with him. But he answered his father, "Listen! For all these years I have been working like a slave for you, and I have never disobeyed your command, yet you have never given me even a young goat so that I might celebrate with my friends. But when this son of yours came back, who has devoured your assets with prostitutes, you killed the fatted calf for him!" Then the father said to him, "Son, you are always with me, and all that is mine is yours. But we had to celebrate and rejoice, because this brother of yours was dead and has come to life; he was lost and has been found."'

LUKE 15:11–32

The soul is symphonic

The parable of the prodigal son in Luke 15 contains a very significant reference to music that is directly related to the concept of God's generosity, grace, mercy and justice. You may not have spotted it, as it goes easily unnoticed. After the younger son has returned home and the father has thrown him a party and a feast, in verse 25 we read: 'Now his elder son was in the field, and as he came and approached the house, he heard music and dancing.'

At first sight there is nothing particularly revealing about this. At a party, one might expect there to be music and dancing. However, it is the language that is used here that is so significant. The Greek word for 'music' in this passage is *symphonias*, which literally means 'together sounding'. The Latin Vulgate version of the Bible has *symphoniam*, meaning 'agreement' or, as it were, 'in tune'.[13] The harmony of the music thereby reflects the harmony of the reunion between father and son within the parable, but it can also represent a wider harmony of that between heaven and earth, between Christ and his church.

One theologian who grasped this concept was St Ignatius of Antioch, when he wrote that the Christian community is like a diverse choir of minds who take their tone from God:

Pray, then, come and join this choir, every one of you; let there be a whole symphony of minds in concert; take the tone all together from God, and sing aloud to the Father with one voice through Jesus Christ, so that He may hear you and know by your good works that you are indeed members of His Son's Body.[14]

The mystic and composer Hildegard of Bingen, writing in 1178, in the 80th year of her life, complains to the prelates of Mainz about the wrongful banning of music in her abbey. Hildegard explains in her letter that music is essential 'not only to… the life of her community, but also its importance both to the wider church and to the world'. The loss of music hindered 'their effort to live in a way that displayed the harmony of the body and soul through their continual singing of praises to God'. She wrote: 'The soul is symphonic' (*symphonalis est anima*).[15] Thus, for Hildegard, her community, and the wider church, was seen as a place where they practiced *symphonia* or *harmonia*. This practice of being 'in tune' with each other is where 'they rehearse living in a way that both their diversity and difference form a pleasing arrangement, an arrangement that not only reflects the celestial harmony of heaven, but also hints at the interplay and mutual indwelling (the counterpoint and harmony) that is the nature of our Triune God'.[16]

Being 'in tune'

The art of being 'in tune' is not just contained within a religious or Christian environment. It was powerfully modelled by Daniel Barenboim, the great Argentinian–Israeli conductor and pianist, and Edward Said, the Palestinian–American scholar, when they founded the West-Eastern Divan Orchestra in 1999. Now based in Seville, this unique orchestra takes musicians from the Middle East, Egypt, Iran, Israel, Jordan, Lebanon, Palestine and Syria. The aim of the orchestra, of course, is primarily to make music, but it also promotes understanding between Israelis and Palestinians. Barenboim says:

> The Divan is not a love story, and it is not a peace story... It's not going to bring peace, whether you play well or not so well. The Divan was conceived as a project against ignorance. A project against the fact that it is absolutely essential for people to get to know the other, to understand what the other thinks and feels, without necessarily agreeing with it. I'm not trying to convert the Arab members of the Divan to the Israeli point of view, and [I'm] not trying to convince the Israelis to the Arab point of view. But I want to... create a platform where the two sides can disagree and not resort to knives.[17]

It is not necessarily easy to produce such harmony out of diversity, to have simultaneous voices which are also one voice. To do so one must

submit one's will to another, staying in tune with one another and sur-
rendering to the music in a way that involves participation, sensitivity
and awareness of others. Even the most diverse voices can be in tune.

At our best as human beings, we begin to join in the symphony and the dance of the divine Trinity of God.

These characteristics of participation, sensitivity and
awareness are also needed
in the work of mercy, which is
why I find music such an apt
metaphor for discussion of our
participation in the work of the Spirit. Music is an enactment of unity
and diversity, harmony and dissonance, where many divergent strands
are held together in a common polyphony of sound. Music, when used
well in worship, prayer and whenever we meet, nearly always brings
people closer, rather than pushing them further away. Music can also
heal, soften, encourage, soothe, inspire, invigorate and harmonise
people. At our best as human beings, we begin to join in the symphony
and the dance of the divine Trinity of God. We are invited and drawn
into the Godhead by his love and grace given freely to us, and it is in
this music and dance that we begin to glimpse the divine. That is why
composers and performers strive for greater perfection of their art,
to bring us closer to the perfect reality of the ultimate harmony: the
three in one. Music, whether performed at a professional level, sung
to oneself or even imagined in one's mind, is, and has always been,
at the heart of the story of faith. When you hear the harmony, melody
and rhythm of music, you might also consider that it is God's gift to
you and his invitation to join him in the symphony and the dance of
the Holy Trinity.

Listening for the melody of mercy

If we are to hear the melodies of God's mercy and justice, we need first
to listen to his voice and tune in to his mercy. In his Nazareth manifesto,
Jesus declares that: 'The Spirit of the Lord is upon me, because he

has anointed me to bring good news to the poor. He has sent me to proclaim release to the captives and recovery of sight to the blind, to set free those who are oppressed, to proclaim the year of the Lord's favour' (Luke 4:18–19). Jesus' response to those most in need was motivated by divine compassion. This is regardless of whether the compassion or mercy is deserved. In fact, any notion that any of us is deserving is absurd. The judgement parable in Matthew 25 shows us that Christ identifies most strongly with the least. In New Testament scholarship there is a divergent interpretation of the term 'the least' in this context. Some scholars believe that Jesus was referring only to the needy among his Jewish brothers and sisters. But we can also interpret this phrase in a universalist sense; that is, those who are the least in our communities, nations and our world – the least affluent, the least cared for, the least loved. Jesus' proximity with the least is so close that Christ is not *like* them, he *is* them. This startling reality begs the question, however, of who are the poor and what exactly is poverty?

Who are the poor?

We can identify at least four main categories of poverty:

- economic poverty – lacking the material means to support themselves to live viably within our society
- relational poverty – lacking a family or community support network to which they can turn in troubled times (family breakdown is a key issue here)
- aspirational poverty – lacking hope or capacity to extricate themselves from the situation they are in
- spiritual poverty – not knowing 'the God of our Lord Jesus Christ, the glorious Father' (Ephesians 1:17, NIV).[18]

These categories are extremely useful for our understanding of a society where power and affluence are the dominant social and political forces. In everyday life we might think we can identify 'the poor' because we imagine them only to be economically disadvantaged. They are the homeless person on the street; they are the struggling unemployed on benefits; they are those who cannot afford the cost of fuel due to the financial climate.

But who of us cannot identify some element of relational poverty in our own lives? Who of us is so content and has such agency that we can aspire and achieve whatever we desire and escape from every unpleasantness of life? And who of us is so in tune with the divine that we can fully boast that we know God in all his ineffability? The works of mercy are not about Christians who 'have everything' giving to those who do not. The gospel tells us that we are all broken and lost. We are all in some way spiritually, relationally and aspirationally poor. And even the well off can be poor in the sense of not using money to do good for others, not being generous and joyful in giving, not offering financial help to those who need it most. There is a kind of poverty in meanness and apathy towards our neighbour.

Responding to the music of God's mercy means listening for his voice, calling each of us to love the stranger and even the enemy, in whom Christ dwells in the depths of the distressed soul. Jesus told a parable about how this might be done.

Who is my neighbour?

An expert in the law stood up to test Jesus. 'Teacher,' he said, 'what must I do to inherit eternal life?' He said to him, 'What is written in the law? What do you read there?' He answered, 'You shall love the Lord your God with all your heart and with all your soul and with all your strength and with all your mind and your neighbour as yourself.' And he said to him, 'You have given the right answer; do this, and you will live.'

But wanting to vindicate himself, he asked Jesus, 'And who is my neighbour?' Jesus replied, 'A man was going down from Jerusalem to Jericho and fell into the hands of robbers, who stripped him, beat him, and took off, leaving him half dead. Now by chance a priest was going down that road, and when he saw him he passed by on the other side. So likewise a Levite, when he came to the place and saw him, passed by on the other side. But a Samaritan while travelling came upon him, and when he saw him he was moved with compassion. He went to him and bandaged his wounds, treating them with oil and wine. Then he put him on his own animal, brought him to an inn, and took care of him. The next day he took out two denarii, gave them to the innkeeper, and said, "Take care of him, and when I come back I will repay you whatever more you spend." Which of these three, do you think, was a neighbour to the man who fell into the hands of the robbers?' He said, 'The one who showed him mercy.' Jesus said to him, 'Go and do likewise.'

LUKE 10:25–37

> **It is through joining in with the melody of God's mercy that we can find depth of meaning in our ordinary, everyday, human experience.**

Who is our neighbour? The one who shows us mercy in times of need; the one to whom we show mercy. In this parable Christ identifies the acts of mercy as a way of expressing love for God and neighbour which leads to eternal life. Compassion, response to need and practical help are directly linked to salvation and love for God. It is through joining in with the melody of God's mercy that we can find depth of meaning in our ordinary, everyday, human experience.

Sounding the depths

What do we mean when we speak about a depth to our lives? The language of depth is the vocabulary we turn to when describing meaningful human experience. As Paul Tillich often suggested:

'Deep' in its spiritual sense has two meanings; it means either the opposite of 'shallow', or the opposite of 'high'. Truth is deep and not shallow; suffering is depth and not height. Both the light of truth and the darkness of suffering are deep. There is depth in God, and there is a depth out of which the psalmist cries to God.[19]

Occasionally, we may describe our experience, our suffering, our joy and our understanding of life as 'profound', which itself comes from the Latin *profundis*, meaning 'deep'. This depth of our everyday experiences and encounters, whether they be suffering or joy, is shared with us by Christ, as expressed in God's self-emptying incarnation, as Karl Rahner realised:

> The eye of faith must see somewhat more deeply into the significance of our everyday, and must perceive in the midst of our everyday lives in their everyday-ness Jesus Christ present in his brothers and sisters.[20]

The parable of the good Samaritan is one that gives us an example of how to live both deep and meaningful lives. 'Which of these three, do you think, was a neighbour to the man who fell into the hands of the robbers?' He said, 'The one who showed him mercy.' Jesus said to him, 'Go and do likewise.'

 A prayer

O God of mercy, we thank you for the inestimable love you give to us in Christ. May we hear the melody of your mercy and tune into the symphonic unity of the Trinity. That humanity, in all its diversity and complexity, may be in harmony with the depth and height of your being and with one another in love. Amen.

Further reading

The Rule of Benedict, ed. Carolinne White (Penguin, 2008).
Mother Teresa, *Essential Writings* (Orbis, 2005).
Jon Sobrino, 'Spirituality and the following of Jesus' in Jon Sobrino and Ignacio Ellacuría (eds), *Systematic Theology: Perspectives from liberation theology* (Orbis, 1993), pp. 233–56.

2

THE SONG OF JUSTICE

> This is what the Lord Almighty said: 'Administer true justice;
> show mercy and compassion to one another. Do not oppress
> the widow or the fatherless, the foreigner or the poor. Do not
> plot evil against one another.'
>
> ZECHARIAH 7:9–10 (NIV)

The works of mercy are not only about compassion and action, they are also about justice for the deprived, whether that deprivation is food, water, shelter, freedom, dignity, home or health. As in the prophecy of Zechariah above, justice, mercy and compassion are commanded by the Almighty in one breath. Throughout history there has been a strong connection between the call for justice and its expression in song: protest songs, freedom songs, laments, celebration and victory songs. In the Old Testament, we are told that music was used by the people of Israel at times of conquest over enemies or persecutors. It was used to lament times when they were in exile in Babylon and for praise, as in Psalm 150, praising God on every instrument. Occasionally, it was used for healing: when Saul suffered from 'the evil spirit from God', perhaps what today we might call depression, he was advised to call upon David, who 'took an harp, and played with his hand: so Saul was refreshed, and was well, and the evil spirit departed from him' (1 Samuel 16:23, KJV). This is what today we might call music therapy.

Music is also documented throughout the New Testament, from the canticles, or songs, sung at the very beginning of the story of the annunciation onwards, through Jesus' life and the story of the early church. One book where music is particularly prominent is the remarkable gospel of Luke. Luke can hardly get through two opening chapters without bursting into song four times in the narrative, with canticles from Mary in the Magnificat ('My soul doth magnify the Lord', Luke 1:46), Zechariah's Benedictus ('Blessed be the Lord God of Israel', Luke 1:68), Simeon's Nunc Dimittis ('Lord, now lettest thou thy servant depart in peace', Luke 2:29) and the angels singing 'Glory to God' (Luke 2:14; all KJV).

All these songs represent a fulfilment of God's promise in Christ, and we might forget, as we sing or listen to one of the many settings of these words at Choral Evensong or Matins, how radical they are in their theology, especially the Magnificat. Mary's words are not just innocent praise. This is singing as radical social commentary – politics, if you like. Mary connects the divine act of the incarnation and her witness to social justice. As Don Saliers puts it, 'To sing with Mary is to sing God's Justice.'[21] Perhaps there is a very relevant point for modern society that a great deal of the music-making surrounding the theme of liberation from oppression in the Bible is sung by women. As Walter Brueggemann writes, Mary's hymn of praise is:

> revolutionary in its world-making… raw in its power… the nations are invited to a new world with a public ethic rooted in and normed by the tales of nameless peasants, widows, and orphans. It is enough to make trees sing and fields clap and floods rejoice and barren women laugh and liberated slaves dance and angels sing.[22]

Mary's song echoes the Old Testament themes of justice too, such as in Hannah's song:

> My heart exults in the Lord;
> my strength is exalted in my God.

My mouth derides my enemies
>   because I rejoice in my victory.
1 SAMUEL 2:1

And in the Psalms:

The Lord brings the counsel of the nations to nothing;
>   he frustrates the plans of the peoples.
PSALM 33:10

In song, Mary highlights the gap between what *is* and what *ought to be* and thus continues the tradition of singing as proclaiming justice and freedom, a tradition which became central to the liberation songs of African–American slaves and their spirituals. When they sang 'Steal away to Jesus' it was not just about focusing on the consolation of their Lord, it was 'code for escape'.[23]

> **This is not justice as government policy or administered by the law courts, but the song of God's dignifying and life-giving, merciful justice.**

To follow Christ means singing songs of justice and peace, proclaiming that there is good news for the poor, release for the captives, freedom for the oppressed. This is not justice as government policy or constructive justice as administered by the law courts, but the song of God's dignifying and life-giving, merciful justice.

Social justice, not just social policy

In his Nazareth manifesto in Luke 4, Jesus proclaims that his life and ministry has, in the words of Bishop David Shepherd's 1983 book, a *Bias to the Poor*: to bring good news to the poor, let the oppressed go free. Echoing the words of Mary's Magnificat, Luke's Jesus proclaims that in the new kingdom of God, 'He has brought down the powerful from their thrones, and lifted up the lowly; he has filled the hungry with good things, and sent the rich away empty' (Luke 1:52–53). Such texts remind us that the good use of power is about empowerment, about enabling others to have agency and dignity, grounded in the truth that we are made in the image of God, loved by God, and that each one of us is unique and beautiful to the one who made us. As God proclaimed: 'Before I formed you in the womb I knew you' (Jeremiah 1:5).

This dignity is also based in solidarity. We belong to each other. Or in the Zulu philosophy of *Ubuntu*, 'I am because we are.' This common humanity leads to a common good in terms of material things. The fruits of the earth are everyone's. As St Ambrose wrote, when you give to the poor, 'you are not making a gift of your possessions to the poor person. You are handing over to them what is theirs.'[24]

Christ's manifesto in Luke's gospel and the command to do works of mercy, found in Matthew's gospel, show us God's bias towards the poor and vulnerable, to whom we respond from a common and God-given human dignity, solidarity and goodness. Therefore, we cannot simply rely on political or social policy to do this work for us, important though that may be. We all have an individual and communal responsibility, following in the footsteps of Christ, to care for the least privileged in our communities.

In John Rawls' 1971 work, *A Theory of Justice*, he argues that benevolence or sentiment are inadequate to bring about social justice. He declares that social justice must be institutional and part of the basic structures of society. It is fundamentally a secular argument that political social justice is the parent to individual acts of social justice. This is based upon two principles, espoused by the German Enlightenment philosopher Immanuel Kant (1724–1804): first, equality of basic liberties and opportunities for self-advancement are more important than social welfare; and second, the distribution of goods and opportunities work to the advancement of all.

However, as Philip Booth has counter-argued, there are problems with placing all our hopes for society in political or capitalist ideologies.

Citing the Catholic document *Gaudium et Spes* ('Joy and Hope'), one of the four constitutions arising from the Second Vatican Council of 1965, Booth quotes: 'The common good embraces the sum of those conditions of the social life whereby men, families and associations more adequately and readily may attain their own perfection' – in other words, bringing the world closer to the perfection of the kingdom of God on earth.[25] Fulfilment and perfection are not subjective categories, he argues, because Christian social justice requires that fulfilment and perfection are found in relationship to God and our relationship with our neighbours. So, while we need social conditions that can bring about the common 'good' for all, Christian social justice is not totally, or even primarily, about policy, because it is more than mere utilitarianism – that is, the greatest good for the greatest number – nor is it about general welfare. It is about human beings taking personal responsibility for caring for each other.

As Booth reminds us, history tells us that millions have died because of nations putting all their trust in centralised systems of government that become totalitarian. Systems that start off with high ideals and great intentions can end up being oppressive and corrupt, as we have seen time and time again in history. And religious institutions can easily have a similar tendency, if given similar autocratic and absolute power. Once an individual delegates responsibility totally to the state or an organised religion, it can lead to corruption. Secondly, handing over responsibility or power to a system denies the fact that doing 'good' is always an individual choice, a personal response to God, and cannot be delegated. It is called free will. And third, asking governments to create systems that provide universal social justice is impossible. There are always unintended consequences of policy, which compromise the success of any system. Social justice is not just a distribution of wealth but actions that contribute towards the common good.

Jesus and justice

The type of social justice this book deals with, the justice of Luke 4 and Matthew 25, is nicely summarised in a Salvation Army booklet called *Jesus and Justice: Living right and righting wrongs*, which states:

> Jesus' mission is captured in a single vision with two dimensions. His hope for a restored humanity envisions well-being for people who are *spiritually poor* and people who are *socially poor*. And in their midst, righteousness and justice mark the events of his days and nights. Jesus lives right and makes life right with others. In Jesus' code, to love is to be just. To be just is to love. And when we claim to follow Jesus we are disciples of justice. Jesus' mission on earth in his time is our mission on earth in our time.[26]

Thus, as John Wesley wrote, we meet Christ when we serve with and get to know people who are suffering. When we go outside our comfort zone, Christ gives us grace. In this uncomfortable place Jesus is our example:

> Jesus' life is a demonstration of how to live and love. Jesus incarnated intentional love. He demonstrated willful, purposeful and creative love; love for God, self, neighbour, truth, righteousness and justice. Jesus envisioned what didn't yet exist. He championed freedom from oppression – discrimination, exclusion, inequality, poverty, sin and injustice.[27]

Thus, Jesus had a vision that the oppressed would be freed and wrongs would be righted where political and legal systems had failed. In this world, in which we still live with visions of hope for a world where dignity and fairness reign, we must imagine it and enact that vision, for we live in the tension of the 'now and the not yet' of God's kingdom.

Justice for the poor

Do you remember the Make Poverty History campaign of 2005? There were global campaigns for trade justice, the wiping clean of certain debts and for better aid. It was a time when people were imagining a better future, and hopeful that it could come about given the right pressure on world leaders. Alas, poverty has not become history and the gap between rich and poor has if anything become wider. One of the main reasons why poverty prevails is because of the apathy of the rich.

In the Acts of the Apostles we do not find the young Christian community apathetic to poverty. Quite the reverse. But what might be surprising is that their response to poverty is not only one of financial recompense, but of justice: 'The embryonic Christian community soon responded to this challenge [of poverty] with melodies of "compassion and action" beginning a radical and sacrificial provision for the poor among them.'[28]

As Gardiner asserts, correcting the wrongs of a society that apathetically allows poverty to persist can be radical and sacrificial. This is why, alongside the compassion of mercy, we need a fire in our bellies that demands justice: 'God is a God of justice… This means that his children are to love justice and hate injustice too… In relation to the poor, it seeks for them not to be disadvantaged due to lack of wealth or status, but to be elevated, valued, and given a voice.'[29]

And so, in addition to the 'constructive justice' of our political and legal systems, we need 'corrective justice'. We have the strength to persist in this practice of corrective, or social, justice, because we are joining in with a work already begun, the music of Christ's melody of mercy, for Christ plays in ten thousand places.

Justice and judgement

If we have justice, we must also have judgement. Reading Matthew 25:31–46, we cannot shy away from it, for Christ speaks about the judgement of the nations and of the kingdom. We cannot ignore that the imagery is stark and apocalyptic, as those who showed mercy are given everlasting heaven and those who did not are condemned to torment. We have talked of God's justice and our own part in social justice. But what about judgement? It is central to the good news, because it leads to mercy, which opens the way to resurrection:

> The good news of Christianity is not that there's no judgement. That wouldn't be good news, because it would mean the oppressed would languish in subjection and wrongdoers would walk unchallenged, free to inflict harm elsewhere. Instead, the good news is that judgement doesn't have the last word. Only after the issuing of the judgement can there be mercy. To exercise mercy doesn't mean not to judge – it means using the power that judgement gives you not to destroy the one judged, but to transform, rehabilitate and repair them… The reason justice is central for Christians is because it is an indispensable stepping-stone on the road to resurrection.[30]

Whether we are considering the world as it is or the kingdom as it might one day be, we are considering community. If we are to sing the song of God's justice, hear the melody of his mercy and practise daily to join in, we need to do it together.

If we are to sing the song of God's justice, hear the melody of his mercy and practise daily to join in, we need to do it together.

There's a song called 'A place at the table', by Shirley Erena Murray and Mary McDonald, which speaks of the kingdom of the now and not yet. It is a vision of the heavenly banquet of God's eternal kingdom, but it also imagines how that might be emulated here and now, with a place at the table for everyone, however 'deserving' or 'undeserving' they might be. The chorus declares that if this happens, then God delights in our being 'creators of justice and joy, compassion and peace'.

 **A prayer**

God of judgement and of mercy, we praise you for the good news you proclaim of justice for the least, the lost and the unloved. May we hear your voice and respond, so that we might sing your song of justice and proclaim the gospel of justice, joy, compassion and peace in our broken world. Amen.

Further reading

Simon Cuff, *Love in Action: Catholic social teaching for every church* (SCM Press, 2019).

John Harvey, *Bridging the Gap: Has the church failed the poor?* (St Andrew's Press, 1987).

Don Saliers, *Music and Theology* (Abingdon Press, 2007).

3

THE CHIMES OF THE CHURCH

■ ■

> We who are called to be poor in spirit, to be fools for Christ,
> who are called to persecution and abuse… in the midst of this
> cheerless and despairing world, we already taste blessedness
> whenever, with God's help and at God's command, we deny
> ourselves, whenever we have the strength to offer our soul for
> our neighbours, whenever in love we do not seek our own ends.
> Mother Maria Skobtsova[31]

In the previous chapter we ended by suggesting that mercy and justice
are actions to be practised together in community. Now we turn to consider how the community of the church might have addressed issues
of social imbalance and injustice in the past and how the church of
today is changing, by means of comparing two approaches to Christian
social action – 'being with' and 'being interrupted' – and suggesting
that there might be an extension to both, which is 'being disrupted'.

Bias to the poor

When I was a teenager, we attended an evangelical Baptist church
on Sundays and not many books written by Anglican church leaders
tended to come across my radar. But one that had captured my parents' imagination, and then mine, was David Sheppard's *Bias to the
Poor*. Sheppard was a slightly romanticised figure in our household,

as he had sacrificed his England cricketing career to enter the church and as bishop of Liverpool had worked brilliantly with ecumenical partners there, especially with the Roman Catholic Archbishop Derek Warlock. *Bias to the Poor* was written from the perspective of Sheppard's experiences of urban deprivation during his ministry and the evidence he found in scripture:

> Bias to the poor sounds like a statement of political preference. My experience has been that some of the most central teachings of orthodox Christianity lead me to this position. I shall argue from Jesus's theme of the Kingdom of God, the calling to the Church to be Catholic, reaching across all human divisions and the doctrine of the Incarnation; they lead me to claim that there is a divine bias to the poor, which should be reflected both in the Church and in the secular world.[32]

Sheppard lived out his beliefs about poverty and tried to shape a church that reached across all human divides. Towards the end of the book, he suggests some ways the church might act:

> What matters is whether those who have eyes to see are presented with authentic signs of God's Kingdom, when they are confronted by the Church. If this is to happen, we need to be the kind of Church which: stays present in the neediest areas and continues to believe and worship; recognises, develops, and supports local ability within the Church and outside it; serves people where they are; tries to understand, and obey the word of God for both rich and poor.[33]

Fifty years on and the face of the Church of England is somewhat different to Sheppard's day, most significantly in human and financial resources. Can the church of 2023 still achieve Sheppard's four objectives?

The church today

In August 2023 *The Times* published the results of a survey which suggested that Britain was no longer a Christian country. The wide-ranging poll found a strong desire among priests for significant changes in the church's teaching on sex, marriage and women's ministry. It also revealed high levels of stress among clergy, partly due to the decline in congregational numbers, but also having to justify the church's traditional teaching in an increasingly secular country.[34]

If our society is becoming less Christian and more sceptical about the church, what approach should the church take when it comes to the poor? In 1983 Sheppard understood that one temptation to be avoided is that of being patronising:

> There is ample evidence to convict the Church of being charitable and paternalistic to the poor… concepts which are rightly to be criticised; both offer help, but frequently retain control in the fatherly or charitable hands of someone else, and therefore may then be said to strengthen rather than weaken dependence. That dependence is the enemy of a true sense of responsibility and self-worth.[35]

If charitable giving can create dependence, it may also be blind to the root causes of poverty that need to be addressed. Mercy, in its fullest sense, requires the transformation of inherently oppressive societal structures. Mere paternalistic charity is not loving, because it is objectivising and manipulative. One way of avoiding such selfishness is attentiveness, meaning 'an active desire for the well-being of the neighbour, and for communion with him or her, based on a recognition of the neighbour's unique worth'.[36] Just as each human is uniquely precious to the one who created them, so recognition of human worth involves a de-centring of ego, of self-dispossession, echoing Christ's own self-emptying through the incarnation. We avoid being charitable exhibitionists, Gustavo Gutiérrez assures us, when we genuinely offer not just bread or water, but the gift of ourselves, a kind of 'authentic love for the poor that is not possible apart from a certain integration into their world and apart from bonds of real friendship with those who suffer despoliation and injustice'.[37]

If we truly give the gift of ourselves, then we must be ready to be challenged and changed. Existing *for* others involves duty and responsibility, but existing *with* others involves relationship. And so we come to the notion of 'being with' as a model for living out lives of mercy, justice and love.

Being with

Samuel Wells has written extensively on this subject. In his thinking and practice he distinguishes between working for, working with, being with and being for. '*Working for* is where I do things and they make your life better', in other words those *with* giving to those *without*. *Working with* 'gains its energy from problem-solving, identifying targets, overcoming obstacles, and fending off the bursts of energy that result'. This 'locates power in coalitions, partnerships, networks. Establishes momentum and empowers the dispossessed', for example, by means of composing systemic structures that contribute to the common good.[38]

Being with 'sees the vast majority of life, and certainly the most significant moments of life, in these terms: love can't be achieved; death can't be fixed; pregnancy and birth aren't a problem needing a solution'. If we try to 'fix' people as problems, it leads to disempowerment and 'reinforces their low social standing'. Wells suggests that 'instead, one must accompany them while they find their own methods, answers, approaches – and meanwhile celebrate and enjoy the rest of their identity that's not wrapped up in what you (perhaps ignorantly) judge to be their problem'.[39]

Being for 'is a philosophy that's more concerned with getting the ideas right, using the right language, having the right attitudes, and ensuring products are sustainably sourced, investments are ethically funded, people are described in positive ways, and accountable public action is firmly distinguished from private consumer choice'.[40] This attitude recognises a need but considers it someone else's responsibility.

Being with recognises people's equal human worth and dignity, it does not patronise or condescend, it is mutual in relationship where giving and receiving can be reciprocal, and it does not pretend that all pain and suffering can be fixed by someone who has apparent 'wealth' of resources. Alas, there is not space in this short book to do justice to 'being with', but it will be an important concept to remember as the rest of this book unfolds.

However, another model, which is critical to some extent of Wells' work, has come from Al Barrett and Ruth Harley, who suggest that we need to do more than 'being with'. We need to be prepared to be 'interrupted', which involves not only coming alongside someone else, but also radically to change ourselves, our behaviour and our preconceptions. It means responding by repenting of our own collusion with corrupt systems that keep others in poverty, repenting of our own apathy and acting sacrificially to make amends for the wrongs we have done.

Being interrupted

The church is not always great at talking about power, especially in its own structures. 'Privilege is powerful precisely because it tends to be invisible to those who have it.'[41] The inability to recognise that power exists even in the most casual of encounters, let alone in more formal ones, is dangerous. Lack of self-knowledge leads to an apathic attitude towards those who do not have power, ensuring the least empowered remain underprivileged. The poor remain poor, the rich

> The inability to recognise that power exists even in the most casual of encounters, let alone in more formal ones, is dangerous.

remain rich. The church is not immune from deluded privilege, so how might the church today fare in terms of self-dispossessive care for the vulnerable?

Well, first, it's possible that it might do better than the wider world, given the church's access to 'the gifts of the Spirit, the wisdom of the Scriptures, the Jesus-shaped habits of our church communities'. Or, second, it could be that the church is 'neatly sealed off from the world'. But a third and 'uncomfortable' possibility is that we Christians are, 'in some ways at least, *more* oblivious than the wider world: that there are aspects of our DNA as Christian communities... that exacerbate certain structural injustices and uphold certain privileges in ways that our wider society is in fact more conscious of, and attempting to deal with, however imperfectly.'[42]

We must be aware that we collude with structural injustices. Moreover, we have inherited, however unconsciously, an imperial legacy of white, male superiority and dominance that must be acknowledged and challenged constantly. Offering a more hopeful solution to the church's blind privilege, Barrett and Harley suggest three 'economies' of church. The first they call 'counting in', which is a traditional model of church growth through efficiency, calculability, predictability and control. This is measurable. The second economy is 'giving out', which involves looking outwards, growing the kingdom outside the church. This involves people from the church going out into the world, but it is a path laden with temptations. Just as Christ was tempted by Satan in the wilderness to do heroic acts of turning stones into bread, performing amazing tricks like throwing himself from a great height or possessing everything he could see, so too the 'heroic saviour' disciple is tempted to be a great provider, performer and possessor. All these heroic acts maintain the centre of power, status and wealth in the giver, and they keep the receiver in a state of disempowerment. These pitfalls echo Sheppard's concerns regarding church paternalism in the 1980s.

A third option is 'being interrupted'. Like 'being with', this is reciprocal and relational, recognising gifts of others, but also allows for a church which is no longer anxious for its own survival, but is prepared to be 'rewilded'.[43] Rewilding looks for gifts in the people within communities, including the residents, as well as the power of local associations, in the resources of the public and volunteer sectors. Rewilding involves listening to the stories and traditions of people in a particular place.[44]

The location of power

So much of Barrett and Harley's thinking is about where power and privilege are located. And this relates particularly to the works of mercy and in helping others. Matthew 25:35–40 raises questions about power and privilege and the nature of Christ. In any act of mercy, where is Christ located in the action? In the giver? In the receiver? Or is there a third option? You may be familiar with these words attributed to Teresa of Ávila:

> *Christ has no body now but yours.*
> *No hands, no feet on earth but yours.*
> *Yours are the eyes with which he looks*
> *with compassion on this world,*
> *yours are the feet with which he walks*
> *to do good,*
> *yours are the hands,*
> *with which he blesses all the world.*

These words firmly *locate* Christ in the giver. He has no hands or feet but yours. Jesus is *in* the person, the actions, the body of the Christian. This is like '*being* Jesus' to those we meet. A second option is taken from Matthew 25:35–40 and Jesus' words about acts of mercy. 'I was hungry' locates Jesus in the neighbour. When we feed someone, we are doing so *to* Jesus. In both the first and the second model, 'the Christian is in the active role, taking the initiative, giving, serving; and the neighbour is in a passive role, on the receiving end, "in need". Both place us, the giver, centre stage. They are paternalistic.'[45] It is at this point that they make a clear distinction between their thinking and that of Wells' 'being with'.[46] It can too easily gloss over those multiple structural injustices in which we're entangled that might well mean, for our neighbours (and many of our Christian siblings within the church too), that attempting to 'be with' them incarnationally – *as God* – is about the last thing that they need.

Therefore, how might we approach these structural injustices as a church and as individuals? Unless we are prepared to be interrupted by being with people, then we are simply 'othering' them and taking a presumptuous and pretentious role as heroic saviour.

Jennifer Harvey would turn our attention towards the example of Zacchaeus and his encounter with Christ. Rather than ask, 'What would Jesus do?', perhaps we should be asking, 'What would Zacchaeus do?' Let's remind ourselves of Zacchaeus's story:

> [Jesus] entered Jericho and was passing through it. A man was there named Zacchaeus; he was a chief tax collector and was rich. He was trying to see who Jesus was, but on account of the crowd he could not, because he was short in stature. So he ran ahead and climbed a sycamore tree to see him, because he was going to pass that way. When Jesus came to the place, he looked up and said to him, 'Zacchaeus, hurry and come down, for I must stay at your house today.' So he hurried down and was happy to welcome him. All who saw it began to grumble and said, 'He has gone to be the guest of one who is a sinner.' Zacchaeus stood there and said to the Lord, 'Look, half of my possessions, Lord, I will give to the poor, and if I have defrauded anyone of anything, I will pay back four times as much.' Then Jesus said to him, 'Today salvation has come to this house, because he, too, is a son of Abraham. For the Son of Man came to seek out and to save the lost.'
>
> LUKE 19:1–10

Zacchaeus' conversion encounter with Christ was radical. As a result, he 'disrupts and reverses the flow of money that had enriched him:

from extracting money from others with ruthless consistency, he now gives it away freely – making reparations to the victims of his exploitation, but also freeing himself from money's stranglehold'.[47] Zacchaeus recognises his own guilt and complicity in a corrupt system and radically changes himself and the nature of his relationship with others. In this instance, the social justice achieved is by changing himself first. This presents us today with a challenge to 'let go of our addictions to being the first to speak or act, central to the story, the heroic providers, performers or possessors'.[48] Those who possess power, due to the privileges of birth, fortune, class, ethnicity, gender or nationality, are to disidentify with a Jesus who might reinforce any of those forms of power. Zacchaeus is a good role model because his encounter with Christ leads to a disentanglement from exploitative structure that gave him wealth, security and status.

In addition to the models of being with and being interrupted, I'd like to offer a third. If we are to 'decentre' both as individuals and as a church, or as communities, and if we are to change for good, then do we not also need an element of disturbance or disruption to the status quo of our old addictions?

Being disrupted

You might think that I'm playing with semantics, and no doubt Barrett and Harley chose their vocabulary with great care. You may think that being 'disrupted' is too strong a word, implying a destructive and negative tendency. But isn't this surely what a complacent society, church and government system needs? Zacchaeus was not interrupted in the sense that it was a temporary change to his routine, after which he returned to his old ways. His whole ethos and practice of living were totally reversed for good. If a TV programme or radio show is 'interrupted', we expect the problem to be sorted out and for normality to resume. Not so with Christ. When Christ healed someone, they stayed healed. They did not resume their blindness after a short interval. Their lives were not interrupted; they were transformed. Christ's death and resurrection did not interrupt the power of guilt and sin to enslave us. They were disrupted, disturbed, so that through him we have salvation and forgiveness, not just for a time but forever.

> Are we willing, in the church, to break down the old structures of hierarchy, pomp, historical power of race, land, finance, abuse, colonialism?

So we too as Christians, asking 'What would Zacchaeus do?', are challenged to be disrupted by our encounters with Christ in the face of our neighbour. Are we willing to be changed forever? Are we willing to consider new ways of living for good? Can we genuinely decentre, dispossess ourselves of pride, so that encounters with others and with Christ might mean re-examining everything we do and everything we own? Are we willing, in the church, to break down the old structures of hierarchy, pomp, historical power of race, land, finance, abuse, colonialism? Are we willing to be a people who say 'Come as you are,' without condition or expectations of respectability as to behaviour? We might say we are, but are we – really? Only when we let go of self can we truly love our neighbour and there find the face of Christ blessing us with his grace, and only then build a just community where everyone is equal.

This poem by Craig Gardiner expresses it beautifully. It's composed around the idea of music, dancing and feasting in the kingdom, as a Come-as-you-are Ceilidh.

The Come-as-you-are Ceilidh
It's a Come-as-you-are Ceilidh,
beginning today around twelve;
They'll be flinging and swinging
to reels of redeeming
where angels will shout
to those inside and out.
The steps of the 'Now and Not Yet'
over flashes of fiddles all dreaming

of grace and abandon,
embraced in the rhythm
of swing and be swung as they come
as they are,
to a come-as-you-are kind of Ceilidh
whose promise sings clearly
of loving more dearly
than any have loved here before.

Now read the poem again. Substitute the word 'church' for Ceilidh. If we can envision that our communities could be like this, then that is the first step towards acting together to make it become a reality. Let's begin that work of imagination now.

A spiritual exercise

Prepare yourself for prayer
Sit comfortably with both feet on the ground and hands open on your lap, as if waiting to receive a gift from God. Let go of your thoughts and worries and entrust yourself and everything to God. Pray that you will be receptive to what God has to say to you in this scripture reading.

Read the passage below out loud, slowly and meditatively. Listen for words or phrases that speak to you. Sit with it for a while.

[Jesus] entered Jericho and was passing through it. A man was there named Zacchaeus; he was a chief tax collector and was rich. He was trying to see who Jesus was, but on account of the crowd he could not, because he was short in stature. So he ran ahead and climbed a sycamore tree to see him, because he was going to pass that way. When Jesus came to the place, he looked up and said to him, 'Zacchaeus, hurry and come down, for I must stay at your house today.' So he hurried down and was happy to welcome him. All who saw it began to grumble and said, 'He has gone to be the guest of one who is a sinner.' Zacchaeus stood there and said to the Lord, 'Look, half of my possessions, Lord, I will give to the poor, and if I have defrauded anyone of anything, I will pay back four times as much.' Then Jesus said to him, 'Today salvation has come to this house, because he, too, is a son of Abraham. For the Son of Man came to seek out and to save the lost.'

LUKE 19:1–10

Meditate
Read these verses again. This time, let the words or phrases that stood out for you the first time become an invitation from God to speak with him. Allow the words to flow through you as you meditate upon them.

Pray
Now read the passage slowly a third time.

Ask
- What is God saying to you in these words?
- What do you want to say to God?
- What feelings are stirred within you?
- Share your answers with God.

Contemplate
Read the text one last time, and this time let the words you have been praying with go free. Be still and at peace with God.

Ask
- What gift has God given you to take away?
- What action might God be inviting you to offer?
- Thank God for this gift and for his invitation.

 **A prayer**

Lord, save us from smug self-reliance and arrogance in our discipleship. Lead us not into the temptation of paternalistic and patronising attitudes. Interrupt our complacency, disrupt our ease, disturb us with your cry of pain at the injustices of the world. Stir us up by the gift of your Holy Spirit to change the unjust structures of our nations, our cities, our churches, our neighbourhoods and our homes. Amen.

Further reading

Jon Sobrino, *The Principle of Mercy: Taking the crucified people from the cross* (Orbis, 1994).

'thirsty, I say to you, as
'gave me drink, you did it to me in prison and you came to me.
the ned me. I was naken you gave me me you clothe
lea was sick and you visited me drink, you and you can
me to me. I was thirsty and you gave you, you me
I was sick and you, as you did it
stranger and you welcomed me, come
'ame to me... Truly, I say to you
ningry an. you did it to me in prison
ned me. I was naken
sick and you visited
I was thir

4

INTERRUPTION, IMPROVISATION AND COMPOSITION: FEEDING THE HUNGRY

'For I was hungry and you gave me food.'
MATTHEW 25:35

As he went ashore, he saw a great crowd, and he had compassion for them, because they were like sheep without a shepherd, and he began to teach them many things. When it grew late, his disciples came to him and said, 'This is a deserted place, and the hour is now very late; send them away so that they may go into the surrounding country and villages and buy something for themselves to eat.' But he answered them, 'You give them something to eat.' They said to him, 'Are we to go and buy two hundred denarii worth of bread and give it to them to eat?' And he said to them, 'How many loaves have you? Go and see.' When they had found out, they said, 'Five, and two fish.' Then he ordered them to get all the people to sit down in groups on the green grass. So they sat down in groups of hundreds and of fifties. Taking the five loaves and the two fish, he looked up to heaven and blessed and broke the loaves and gave them to

his disciples to set before the people, and he divided the two fish among them all. And all ate and were filled, and they took up twelve baskets full of broken pieces and of the fish. Those who had eaten the loaves numbered five thousand men.
MARK 6:34–44

The first of our works of mercy is about feeding the hungry. To help us explore this I'm going to use three descriptive terms from the world of music.

The first musical term is *interruption*. We have already considered interruption as an important way in which our preconceptions and addictive behaviour of retaining and misusing power are challenged. In music the interrupted cadence is a harmonic sequence that brings a phrase or a piece to an end. Rather than finishing with a feeling of homecoming, however, it ends with a sense of unease, that the work is not yet complete, and that there is a need for another ending that will help the listener to feel a sense of satisfaction. In the work of social action, we often feel that our work is never complete, that it is interrupted, unfinished, unsatisfactory. But being interrupted can also be a positive characteristic of the works of mercy. It is only through interruption that sometimes a person's need comes to our attention. If we were never interrupted by events and people's daily lives, we could never tune in to their song, their melody.

The second musical metaphor is *improvisation*, the creative, responsive and spontaneous style of music that is created or composed freely in the moment, sometimes as a single player or singer, and sometimes in a group, where musicians can respond to each other's creative impulses and bring their own offering into the musical mix. Improvisation requires imagination and a willingness to 'let go' of control and allow the music to flow out. In this chapter there are stories of people's creative responses to situations or needs, in which empathy with another human being has invoked a resonance, which sounds in the hearts of those who feel the impulse to respond and to come alongside another person.

And the third metaphor is *composition*. It involves a more studied and considered form of creativity than improvisation. It is not just resonating with the needs of the moment, but seeks to produce a system, a written 'score', which becomes the map for each member of the organisation or community to follow. In musical terms, a composition can take each individual player of the symphony orchestra and weave their melodies into the harmony of the whole. In terms of the works of mercy, a composition can be the template that creates years of systemic common good. This could be anything from an informal community initiative, to a church-organised system of social action, to a registered national charity. There are many forms.

In the famous story of the feeding of the five thousand from Mark's gospel, Jesus is interrupted, he improvises and he composes. He is interrupted by the need of the crowd. He resonates with their need and considers a response. If he decides to send them home, some of them will faint on the way. So, he decides to improvise. Like a jazz musician taking the fragments of a tune and weaving around them a musical tapestry of beauty and light, Jesus takes the fragments of food and creates a great feast. He is inspired in the moment with so much generosity of spirit that everyone is full of food and the grace of the divine. But Jesus is also a composer of a great symphony of riches. He has fed the crowd and the disciples with knowledge, with wisdom in his teachings, with food for their bodies and grace for their souls. Out of little has come something rich. I like to think that, after such a blessed banquet, some of those present may well have burst into song.

> **Hunger and unhappiness are the creative impulses that lead to compassionate action.**

Here's another story of interruption, improvisation and composition that has led to many inspired projects which have fed the hungry over many years. The initial impetus, as we shall see, was personal suffering and need as a child. Hunger and unhappiness are the creative impulses that lead to compassionate action. Sharon's life, as you will see below, was *interrupted* by shattering events; she *improvised* to respond to an urgent need; and she used that improvisation to *compose* something lasting for her community.

SHARON'S STORY

I didn't get fed as a kid – as simple as that. I was hungry as a child. In fact, my mother was mentally unwell. She not only neglected me, but she actively tried to harm me so that I was often very sick. So now I can't bear the idea of hungry families. No child should be hungry, and I do what I can to make sure no child is. My father sent me to a minor public school to try to make a lady out of me. He wanted me to get a decent education but didn't realise it was not a good school. When I left school, I ended up eating in a working men's club, as I needed food. The cook asked me if I wanted to work in the kitchen. It was a comforting place when home was not. This led to me taking a home economics course and working in a kitchen in a school. But then I had the chance to train as a teacher. When I finished teacher training in 1974, the government raised the school leaving age from 15 to 16, which created a lot of fed-up teenagers. But I loved teaching them and we did unusual things, like build an allotment around the school. I didn't mind if they mucked about. We were having fun. They expected me to bollock them, but I didn't. Every year the head teacher gave me a different challenge. I did a lot of work with carers and free school meals.

Interruption

After 30 years of teaching, I was diagnosed with Parkinson's disease and left with a good pension, so I set up a food business. I took out a £375,000 loan from the bank and started a cake-making company, manufacturing thousands of cakes for supermarkets, working the staff in three shifts per day. It was a phenomenal success until the recession and the bank foreclosed on the loan and I had to pay it back immediately. I couldn't protect myself. I put the company into liquidation and couldn't trade for two years. I paid everybody what they were due. I sold my home, and everything went.

So, I said to myself, 'There you go! Now's your chance to start again.' I was sofa surfing for two years and doing odd jobs. I raised enough money to put a deposit on a house and bought one in Margate, where I started a little artisan food company called Bar Fifteen, where I produced cereal bars from home with only 15 ingredients.

When that company ended, I was going to retire. And that's when I found myself sitting on a bus, thinking, 'This retirement thing is a bit dull.' I couldn't see out, as the windows were steamed up. All the passengers were sort of isolated in the space. Then this mother said to her young daughter, 'Do you want to know what we're going to have for tea?' and all the passengers listened eagerly to hear what they were going to have. Then she said, 'Hot dogs, alphabet potatoes and scotch pancakes,' and everyone on the bus went, 'Ugh!' You can't eat that sort of rubbish every day. Nevertheless, she was a hero, like lots of mums, doing her best. I don't have many lightbulb moments, but I suddenly realised what she needed. She needed somewhere she could go where she would be welcome, where her choice would be limited and cheaper and better, and she would learn things along the way. I jumped off the bus, went and bought her ingredients for a healthy meal, and she fed her family for 50 pence that day.

Improvisation

It took me a few years to achieve what I wanted to do, because nobody could see it. Nobody will give you money for the twinkle in your eye. But I started Our Kitchen as a pop-up activity, and we carried everything as we went. Then the pandemic happened in

2020, and I set up what people call a 'hub and spoke' operation. First, I did a breakdown of the area and worked out where all the food banks were. I set up six new food banks and put them in the geographical gaps. I got £82,000 from the Department for Environment, Food and Rural Affairs and that kept some local food providers going through the pandemic as I bought from them.

The town clerk at Ramsgate gave me the use of trucks and drivers, who took the food out from the old fire station to deliver tens of thousands of parcels of fresh food. It was fabulous. The building was free, and everything was going in the right direction.

In August 2020 schools started going back, and I realised we had done much too good a job, as we had lots of people dependent on free food. Then someone from Thanet District Council offered me a shop in Margate. So, we took over an old hairdresser's shop and distributed food.

Composition

It's an interesting business model. You must take each product and pitch the price just right. I worked out that if we could keep our costs really low: no rent, no wages, running on volunteers to start with, then the money we earned from the food would probably be enough to buy in the next load of food. It is all about volume. If you sell the food cheaper, they can buy more. It is not a food bank. If you give something to somebody, you don't get it right. By getting it wrong you undermine that person. You imply that the family should be something that they're not. That they should know what to do with bloody chickpeas. But if you let them choose themselves and support them in that choice, then you have a collaborative approach. One of our mums was on *You and Yours* on BBC Radio 4 talking about Our Kitchen. And she said, 'I was frightened of butternut squash when I first went, but thanks to Sharon, now I'm not frightened of it.'

We have 4,000 families registered with Our Kitchen in Margate and Ramsgate. We tried an electronic registration system, but it was rubbish. People are fed up with giving their details to computers and fed up with giving their personal information to the government. So we now have a blank piece of paper, and we write down what people are willing to tell us and how we can help them.

What I do is so simple. My children despair of me, but it's how I want to live my life. Our Kitchen was bought by Social Enterprise Kent and is now run by them. Now, I use school kitchens to provide more food. All over the country there are cooks working in school kitchens. So I pay school cooks to stay after school for a couple of hours, use the school kitchen (with the consent of the school, of course) and make healthy meals to pack into boxes and put into microwavable containers which can be returned and reused. It's a low-cost model again. All I am doing is using the expertise of the cooks for a couple of hours a day. That costs me about £50 a day or £250 a week. They have got to hack me out a load of food for that. Then the volunteers go in and sterilise, pack the food, label it and freeze it down. The volunteers also prep the fruit and veg for the next day. I give the school fresh fruit and veg for their school meals the next day. The volunteers have all their food hygiene qualifications but do not go into the kitchen. It is a high-speed operation. I am making no dividing line between the food for the school meals and the frozen meals. You must sell cheap. £1.20 per meal. Decent food.

And my meals are not just going to the school families: anybody can be eligible to have one if they have a need. Families do not come to the school to collect meals. The outlet is a library, where the meals are in a new freezer. The library also acts as a warm space for those who are struggling to heat their homes. In a few years, when we persuade ourselves that we are out of recession and are wealthy again, we will have set up successful local food production. I am beavering away and feeding thousands of people. And I need funding from councils, charities and anyone who can give me a grant.

It's psychologically important that families can put roast meat on the table on Christmas Day. So we have created a meal with good-quality chicken thigh, stuffing, bacon, veg and sauces. It looks like the plumpest, most delicious Christmas dinner, and these sell at £1 per meal and take 40 minutes to heat up.

It's so simple. I have a robust relationship with the local authorities. But I have a wonderful relationship with them.

— — — — — — — — — — — —

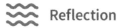 **Reflection**

- In your own life, have there been times when your own suffering has become a source of compassion for others? If so, what was your response?
- What does Sharon do differently from the food banks, and why?
- Has your life ever been seriously interrupted? In what way? How did you respond?

The next story is directly related to Sharon's story, because Matt ran a community meal in a parish hall, leading a team of volunteers using food from Our Kitchen. As the community meal was already established when Matt joined, its composition was already in place. However, to lead it, Matt has found that improvisation and variations of the composition have been necessary to keep it running well.

MATT'S STORY

— — — — — — — — — — — —

I wasn't always a volunteer or running a community meal. I did a degree in accountancy and law and began training as a chartered accountant before hating the work and dropping out. I went temping in the city and stumbled across an agency stockbroker. They offered me a full-time position and a year later, after several successful trips around Europe and Hong King, I found myself sitting on the trade floor. They were a very small broker doing ten trades a day and became the world's largest agency broker and listed on NASDAQ. I didn't like the day-to-day work and was only really doing it for the money. I did, however, really like the people I worked with, who were almost a family, and still meet up with them today.

Interruption

I took redundancy in 2013 and sadly lost my wife in 2014. She passed away suddenly, and I was left with two kids. I had a life insurance pay-out and became a full-time parent. I needed to fill my time when the girls were at school and briefly tried being a school governor.

Then I met my second wife, Sue, and moved to Monkton in Thanet, close to Minster. I started doing an admin role in the church, arranging weddings, etc. I got friendly with the vicar through Sue volunteering as a church warden. I am not a Christian but liked working within a group of nice people. I did try going back to work but now have got into a habit of not working and I don't need to work. But then I saw an advert for volunteers in a weekly church programme.

The composition

I volunteered at St George's Community Meal, serving food to the homeless and vulnerable people. Then I was asked to run it. We registered it with the district council and went through all the paperwork. Now we have a good group of volunteers. We use Our Kitchen, who run a shop out of the hall. We use their food, and they cook for us and do all the preparation. This week they had a lot of pumpkins, so they did a nice pumpkin curry bake and pumpkin mash. We use fresh food ingredients, which is good for the guests. We had a record number of guests this week (44), so it was a busy week with lots of social issues going on. We try to focus on just feeding people and having a good and relaxed evening. We're not social workers or police; we ask people to leave their 'baggage' at the door, and we need to keep the volunteers safe. We have a good routine now and the efforts of everyone have been incredible.

Improvisation

We have a lot of homeless people coming along now and people with mental health issues. We do get some tension sometimes with the groups so have changed the layout of the tables, so people don't have to look at each other who don't want to. We haven't banned individuals or groups from coming to the meal as all need to eat, irrespective of behaviour. If there are problems, then we can sit people with volunteers and separate those who have issues with each other. We try to lighten the evening by having a quiz. With increased cost of living and poverty, tensions can run a bit high, but the food is incredible and goes down well every single week. The cooks mix up the recipes each week and change the menus.

We're getting to a point now where we might need to ask people to book or to have two sittings. We have lots of people coming in with alcohol issues, but if they are sitting down and behaving that's fine. We have some loud people, and we acknowledge that, but we also ask them to be respectful of others.

It can be exhausting. I struggled initially helping people who are dealing with hunger and poverty and then going home myself to a warm, safe home. But once you get over that initial phase, it is rewarding and good fun. There are lots of people who want to give money or a small donation for their meal and we have taken donations occasionally to help fund the project. If you can sit down and treat people as human beings on the same level with you, we find this works best. Some people don't want to work with folk who might have some mental health problems or even some hygiene issues, so the choosing of volunteers is important.

In my opinion, there is always going to be a door to open in life that, if we go through it, we can end up where these people are, or go through another door and we get the best life ever. But if opportunity doesn't come knocking you have to start by building the door yourself.

We all work together as a team. We all have different backgrounds and life experience, but we all come together for a single aim. If I didn't enjoy it, I wouldn't do it. You don't feel like you're running a team, you feel like part of a team. Sometimes you go home feeling a little despondent, but we all have a bad day at work sometimes.

I'm not expecting a reward or anything. I do it because I've been very lucky. I struggle with injustice in the world. A lot of people blame religion for wars, but I always say it is greed and power that drive people and then they use religion as an excuse to justify their behaviour. For me, it's easier to say that what I do is try to help others, but I don't need to justify it by saying that I have a religion. It's easy to say that if you believe in God then you will have all the riches you need; but, for me, it's not true.

At the meal we still say grace, and there is a little talk about Jesus, faith, God, which is given by one of the other volunteers. Some guests leave at that point and then come back. I don't personally object to anyone who has faith. If a person is helping to change the world, it makes no difference to me whether they believe that it is God helping this to happen. There are guests who have faith, and I would love to have faith, but I can't get my head around it and you can't force yourself to believe in it. For me there is too much social injustice in the world motivated by greed and money for the existence of a God and a faith. In my opinion, having a faith won't change the lives of the people we work with; only they can.

The work itself can be highly rewarding and as I walk around Ramsgate, I bump into so many people who come to the meal and chat with them. There is a real sense of a community within the group.

— — — — — — — — — — —

 ## Reflection

- Matt has no Christian faith. Is he fulfilling Jesus' command to do works of mercy?
- Where do you think Christ might be in the community meal?
- What privileges, or deprivations, were you born into?
- Matt talks about the door of opportunity. How could you create a door of opportunity for yourself? And how for others?

Matthew's view of church and religion raises an issue around what our motivations are for helping those in need and contributing to the common good. Liz Rook runs a community larder at All Saints Church in Canterbury, offering food, hospitality, welcome and help in a warm and safe space every Friday. She asks, 'What are the needs of those who feed the hungry? Why do we do what we do? And what are the needs of those of us who serve our friends each week through the All Saints community larder?' The answer to her own questions proves interesting and challenging reading.

LIZ'S STORY

— — — — — — — — — — —

I've always been quite challenged in my Christian faith by a parable that Jesus tells in which he speaks about people who are hungry and thirsty (Matthew 25:35–40). As volunteers at the Breakfast Club and Community Larder at All Saints Church Canterbury, we certainly need compassion, understanding and flexibility. We need wisdom, and a willingness to come alongside people. We need knowledge of the current pressures in society and a willingness to keep informed about these and updated. We also need a non-judgemental attitude.

Northgate Ward, which is where our church is, is one of the poorest in the city, with child poverty rates higher than in many London boroughs. It's the place where life expectancy is reduced by up to ten years compared with other boroughs or wards in our area, a fact confirmed in the recently produced report by the Sustainable Development Goals on poverty in Canterbury.[49]

We have around 20 volunteers in the community larder; not all profess to be Christians, but we do need all who join us to be sympathetic to the Christian faith. Those of us who are Christians have a definite desire to see everyone come to know Jesus as their friend and Saviour, whoever they are, wherever they're from. We believe that people should see in the love and care shown on Friday at All Saints something of the love of God. We want folks to know there's no distinction between guests and volunteers. We are all made in the image of God, a God who loves us. And we want people to know that we serve them because we know Jesus who served and loved everyone.

So, should we be encouraging the Friday Community Larder guests to come to church? Liz replied:

Well, if the church is the body of Christ, our prayer is that for now, Friday can be part of our friends' experience of what church is. As they get to know us, as they build relationships with us, our prayer is that we might slowly but surely help people to want to know more about the God we serve, who makes such a difference in our lives.

Steve Sjorgen wrote a book called *Conspiracy of Kindness*.[50] He started a church in Cincinnati, Ohio. It grew to an attendance of 7,000 people. Their motto is 'Small things done with great love are changing the world.' They carry out random acts of kindness, like paying for a stranger's coffee or writing a thank you note to a shop assistant. Kindness is showing God's love in practical ways. They've discovered the power of kindness to effect positive change, both in their lives and the lives of the people around them.

> **Unexpected kindness is the most powerful, least costly, and most underrated agent of human change.**

Unexpected kindness is the most powerful, least costly, and most underrated agent of human change. When kindness is expressed, healthy relationships are created, community-to-community connections are made and nourished, and people are inspired to pass on kindness. This is our experience. And we thank God for this amazing opportunity which has come out of a very difficult period in our society, post-Covid, and in the context of the ongoing cost-of-living crisis. If we can be anything, let's be kind. For surely kindness is a fruit of the Holy Spirit. And it is so closely linked with the acts of mercy. Proverbs says, 'Blessed is the one who is kind to the needy' (Proverbs 14:21, NIV).

May God bless us as we honour him, by prioritising the poor and showing kindness to those in need.

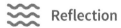 Reflection

- Liz is motivated by the challenge of Matthew 25 and her faith. How important is that to you?
- Liz said, 'There's no distinction between guests and volunteers. We

are all made in the image of God, a God who loves us.' How can you come alongside someone today and be with them as an equal before God?

- Are the works of mercy also works of evangelism?

Liz works closely with Helen, who leads a small community. Here's her story.

HELEN'S STORY

I recently retired from full-time secondary teaching of religious studies. We're told on numerous occasions that Jesus had compassion. Compassion isn't just feeling sorry for people; it's to recognise the need and to help the situation. We're all aware of the cost-of-living crisis and the rise of energy prices. But I didn't fully understand how far this stretched. Last week I was watching the news, and it was a story about the effect of Covid-19 in Bolton, which was one of the areas with the most Covid cases, but also the lowest take-up for vaccines. One reason for this was the high number of people on zero-hour contracts. So, if they missed work to go to a vaccine appointment, they wouldn't get paid. That shocked me; it horrified me. It's something that I really couldn't comprehend at all. I knew that people weren't having vaccines because of stories they'd heard. But it never occurred to me that people wouldn't take a vaccine because of pay. The cost-of-living crisis is affecting everyone. But for some, it isn't a matter of living well; it's a matter of living full stop. And this is where Connecting Canterbury tries to step in to help in these situations.

I started volunteering about 20 months ago, and I became a team leader in February 2023. But what is it? It's part of the Social Justice Network, and we currently offer three main services: emergency energy grants; applying for various grants, including through Acts 435[51] applications; and signposting, form-filling and connecting people with various services that they need. We also work alongside Citizens Advice, which has been an absolute lifesaver. We started in 2016, and it has evolved quite significantly since then with the needs of the communities. Originally, there was much more of a focus on banking and saving with Kent Savers, which is a credit union, in response to the Archbishop of Canterbury's criticisms of Wonga and other payday loans companies, which you might remember. Payday loans led to people ending up with considerably more debt than they could pay back. Kent Savers allows people to save and to receive loans at an affordable rate.

For energy, most of our clients use prepayment meters. So, when they come to us, they're often already in an emergency. They are so grateful for any help they can receive. Many people that we speak to apologise to us because they don't like asking for help. But it's got to that point where they realise they need help and they need to find somewhere to be able to access that help. In the winter months, people were choosing whether to have heating or whether to feed their children or go hungry themselves. They would often rely on services offered by school, such as breakfast clubs, free school meals or Make Lunch,[52] to ensure their children ate, because they didn't have the fuel to be able to use the oven as well as heat the house, have showers, half baths, etc.

In 2022 we distributed £9,120 to 562 people. Some of those people would have received more than one grant throughout the year. And between January and April of this year, we have so far distributed £2,575 to 170 different people.

The second thing we do is to apply for grants for household items. We mainly do this through Acts 435 for free, which is a charity set up by John Sentamu, former Archbishop of York. It's based on Acts 4:35, where they distributed to each as any had need. I love this focus of sharing resources, and that anyone can receive through a network of churches across the UK, as well as individual posts on their website. People can apply for grants to help with a variety of needs. It's possible to help specific needs that are posted on the website. We act as advocates, applying for grants for people needing white goods, beds and carpets, among other items. We can apply for grants of up to £200. In 2022, we gave around 80 grants, but now we find a significant rise in people coming to us for these grants. When people move into social housing, there is often nothing in the house. It is a concrete shell with no carpets, no beds, no washing machine. £200 helps to start furnishing the property. It won't pay for everything, of course, so we must work out, with them, what's most important at that point.

— — — — — — — — — — — —

 Reflection

- How has the cost of living crisis affected you or those you know?
- Is the work of Connecting Canterbury, and other charities, compensating for the deficiencies in government provision and social policy?
- Have you ever had to choose between heating or eating?

Coda: are you hungry?

So far in this chapter we have considered how we might be interrupted, improvise and compose creatively in resonance with those fellow human beings who are our neighbours. Samuel Wells presents us now with a question: are you hungry? If so, what kind of hunger do you have? 'There are two kinds of hunger,' he writes. 'There's a hunger that has a name. It's a hunger where you know what you want but you haven't got it or can't have it: when you interviewed for a job, and you can't understand why they didn't appoint you… But there's another kind of hunger. It's a hunger that lingers deep, disturbingly, in the bottom of your soul, but it doesn't have a name.'[53] This is a challenge to all

Christian believers. When we are engaged with love for our neighbour in feeding those who are hungry, do we stop to consider what kind of hunger we are feeding?

This work of mercy of feeding the hungry lifts our minds, hearts and souls from the material and physical to the divine. Our hunger for life and fulfilment is a relational response to a God who is 'hungry' for us. This is like a musical discovery that draws us together in one song:

> God's hunger is greater than ours. But God knows what that hunger is for. It's for us. And discovering that is for us like discovering choral music... It unearths a gift that was longing to get out. For others, it's a realization that together we can make something beautiful we could never make alone, that there's a place for all shapes and sizes and voices and energies in a song that takes all our energies to make but comes from a force much bigger than us.[54]

The good news of the gospel is that there is living bread in the life of Jesus Christ, in whom all our hungers are satisfied. Like a musical phrase that dies away into silence, leaving the listener craving for more, all our hungers in this life are only ever satiated temporarily. Listen to the music of God's melody and you will hear music that sings of eternal love.

 **A prayer**

Miraculous God, who created us in all our physical, mental and spiritual beauty, we thank you for the gift of food and the abundance of your provision for us. May we share the good fruits of this world with those in need, and help to nourish one another in body, mind and spirit, as we celebrate the wonder of your hunger for us in the love of Jesus Christ, our Lord. Amen.

 A spiritual exercise

Prepare yourself for prayer
Sit comfortably with both feet on the ground and hands open on your lap as if waiting to receive a gift from God. Let go of your worries or thoughts and entrust yourself and everything to God. Pray that you will be receptive to what God has to say to you in this scripture reading.

Read the passage below out loud, slowly and meditatively. Listen for words or phrases that speak to you. Sit with it for a while.

> The next day the crowd that had stayed on the other side of the sea saw that there had been only one boat there. They also saw that Jesus had not gotten into the boat with his disciples but that his disciples had gone away alone. But some boats from Tiberias came near the place where they had eaten the bread after the Lord had given thanks. So when the crowd saw that neither Jesus nor his disciples were there, they themselves got into the boats and went to Capernaum looking for Jesus.
>
> When they found him on the other side of the sea, they said to him, 'Rabbi, when did you come here?' Jesus answered them, 'Very truly, I tell you, you are looking for me not because you saw signs but because you ate your fill of the loaves. Do not work for the food that perishes but for the food that endures for eternal life, which the Son of Man will give you. For it is on him that God the Father has set his seal.' Then they said to him, 'What must we do to perform the works of God?' Jesus answered them, 'This is the work of God, that you believe in him whom he has sent.' So they said to him, 'What sign are you going to give us then, so that we may see it and believe you? What work are you performing? Our ancestors ate the manna in the wilderness, as it is written, "He gave them bread from heaven to eat."' Then Jesus said to them, 'Very truly, I tell you, it was not Moses who gave you the bread from heaven, but it is my Father who gives you the true bread from heaven. For the bread of God is that which comes

down from heaven and gives life to the world.' They said to him, 'Sir, give us this bread always.'

Jesus said to them, 'I am the bread of life. Whoever comes to me will never be hungry, and whoever believes in me will never be thirsty. But I said to you that you have seen me and yet do not believe. Everything that the Father gives me will come to me, and anyone who comes to me I will never drive away, for I have come down from heaven, not to do my own will but the will of him who sent me. And this is the will of him who sent me, that I should lose nothing of all that he has given me but raise it up on the last day. This is indeed the will of my Father, that all who see the Son and believe in him may have eternal life, and I will raise them up on the last day.'

JOHN 6:22–40

Meditate

Read these verses again. This time, let the words or phrases that stood out for you the first time become an invitation from God to speak with him. Allow the words to flow through you as you meditate upon them.

Pray

Now read the passage a third time, slowly.

Ask

- What is God saying to you in these words?
- What do you want to say to God?
- What feelings are stirred within you?
- Share your answers with God.

Contemplate

Read the text one last time, and this time let the words you have been praying with go free. Be still and at peace with God.

Ask
- What gift has God given you to take away?
- To what action might God be inviting you?
- Thank God for this gift and for his invitation.

Further resources

Acts 435, **acts435.org.uk**

Catholic Relief Services, 'Live Mercy: Feed the hungry', **crs.org/sites/
default/files/usops-resources/live_mercy_feed_the_hungry.
pdf**

Martin Charlesworth and Natalie Williams, *A Church for the Poor:
Transforming the church to reach the poor in Britain today* (David
Cook, 2017).

Tim Chester, *Unreached: Growing churches in working-class and
deprived areas* (InterVarsity Press, 2012).

Make Lunch, **tlg.org.uk/get-involved/tlg-corporate-partnerships/
corporates-make-lunch**

Social Enterprise Kitchen, **sekgroup.org.uk/support/support-for-
people/se-kitchen**

Natalie Williams and Paul Brown, *Invisible Divides: Class, culture and
barriers to belonging in the church* (SPCK, 2022).

5

RELATIONSHIP, RESONANCE AND REFRESHMENT: GIVING DRINK TO THE THIRSTY

■ ■ ■ ■ ■ ■ ■ ■ ■ ■ ■ ■ ■ ■ ■ ■ ■ ■

'I was thirsty and you gave me something to drink.'
MATTHEW 25:35

[Jesus] came to a Samaritan city called Sychar, near the plot of ground that Jacob had given to his son Joseph. Jacob's well was there, and Jesus, tired out by his journey, was sitting by the well. It was about noon.

A Samaritan woman came to draw water, and Jesus said to her, 'Give me a drink'. (His disciples had gone to the city to buy food.) The Samaritan woman said to him, 'How is it that you, a Jew, ask a drink of me, a woman of Samaria?' (Jews do not share things in common with Samaritans.) Jesus answered her, 'If you knew the gift of God and who it is that is saying to you, "Give me a drink," you would have asked him, and he would have given you living water.' The woman said to him, 'Sir, you have no bucket, and the well is deep. Where do you get that living water? Are you greater than our ancestor Jacob, who gave us the well and with his sons and his flocks drank from it?' Jesus said to her, 'Everyone who drinks of this water will be thirsty again, but those who drink of the water that I will

give them will never be thirsty. The water that I will give will become in them a spring of water gushing up to eternal life.' The woman said to him, 'Sir, give me this water, so that I may never be thirsty or have to keep coming here to draw water.'
JOHN 4:5–15

How precious is your steadfast love, O God!
   All people may take refuge in the shadow of your wings.
They feast on the abundance of your house,
   and you give them drink from the river of your delights.
For with you is the fountain of life;
   in your light we see light.
PSALM 36:7–9

In the story about Christ and the Samaritan woman at Jacob's well, there is refreshment, relationship and resonance. The refreshment is not only provided by the water of the well, for Jesus is thirsty for some water, but the woman has a thirst for something she cannot yet name, the living water springing up to eternal life, which is to be found in the person and salvation of Christ himself. There is relationship, as their banter soon turns to a serious invitation to drink from divine springs of life. And there is resonance as, in the verses that follow the passage quoted above, the woman understands Christ's insights about her own life and circumstances and proclaims these to her community, inviting them to come and see the Messiah who 'told me everything that I have ever done!' (John 4:29). The result of her evangelism is the conversion of many of her neighbourhood to believe in Christ. The meeting of Jesus and the Samaritan creates a resonance that is felt far and wide, first in Samaria and then to the whole world through the word of God, as related by John.

The meeting of Christ with this woman is like a musical duet, with theme and counter melody weaving together in their exchanges. In music we also find relationships and resonance. It is the relationship between the notes and the silence between the notes and chords that turn mere sound into music, as pitches, melodies and harmonies relate to one another. Then there are the human relationships involved in music, between composer and the music composed, between the creator and the created; between the composer, who imagines the music, and the performer, who enables the music to come to life; and between the composer, performer and recipient, the audience or listener. For music to work it must be resonant. We hear the resonance of a single instrument or voice as the sound waves ripple outwards into space and time. We hear the human resonance between singers and players, an understanding between violinist and cellist, between soprano and baritone, who embody the sounds and bring the music, as intended by the creative composer, into being. There is reciprocity, a mutual give and take with each musician within a group, and empathy too in the making and receiving of music. If there is not, then music cannot happen. If we cannot listen to one another, we cannot hear how to respond – how to adapt our own voice, in dynamics, pitch, tone, volume, colour or strength.

So the metaphor of music and the biblical narrative of Jacob's well become useful ways of exploring our second work of mercy – giving drink to the thirsty: both those who are physically thirsty, but also those who are thirsty for company, friendship, respect, dignity, help, comfort, purpose, meaning and ultimately refuge, redemption and peace. We're now going to hear Patrick's story and how he and his wife Debbie responded to the needs of the thirsty in their community and thereby created beautiful relationships and a refuge, the results of which have resonated far beyond their locality, helping many people to find their own voice.

PATRICK'S STORY

Cliftonville in Margate is one of the poorest parishes in the country. Many people are either drug- or alcohol-dependent; they may be ex-offenders, have mental health issues or be street homeless or sofa surfers. A significant number of people are also vulnerable in lots of other ways. They may have learning difficulties; they may be recent care leavers. Cliftonville is a hard place to live. During our time at St Paul's Church, where Debbie and I ministered, our hearts were often broken by the encounters and the experiences we had with the people of this parish, because the reality is that sharing life with people doesn't usually fit into tidy boxes. It's messier than that. It's even more dangerous than that sometimes.

Having our hearts broken wasn't a bad thing. Our tendency is to shy away from that kind of pain. We don't naturally want to have our hearts broken, but it grew compassion in us. For example, I knew a guy who, years ago, lived in a tiny flat for 17 years. And for most of that time, he had lived without any running water. The taps and pipes were there, but they didn't work. Why? Because he was too scared to complain to the landlord, who had a reputation for answering complaints with a baseball bat. Eventually, with our help, the tenant managed to get into other accommodation. Sadly, he committed suicide in the isolation and loneliness of the Covid lockdown. Even now, I personally know of at least two other people who do not have running water in modern accommodation.

> **Having our hearts broken wasn't a bad thing. Our tendency is to shy away from that kind of pain... but it grew compassion in us.**

Other people, who are rough sleepers, perhaps dossing down on a bench or if they're lucky, in a tent, would come and get water from the church's outdoor tap just to be able to wash themselves or to get a drink. These are third-world problems in a first-world country. There is something within us that wants to help the person in the gutter. Regardless of our own character, because we are not saints, you can't work in this environment for long and not want to help the stranger or the person who has no running water or electricity or food or school uniform for their child. Even if all you can offer is a listening ear for five minutes or to say, 'You are loved and welcome.' Or it might mean working with someone for years and years, taking one step forward and one step back.

Relationship

We think that church should be about belonging first, before belief and behaviour. So everyone is invited to feel that they belong. But we have encountered a lot of behaviour over the years that most people would not consider normal in church, such as violence and substance abuse. In terms of how to deal with that, we wrote the book as we went along. In the first year or two we found it hard. Verbal violence, abuse, fights in the church, drug-taking, prostitutes outside the church. We took the view, and still do, that no one will ever fall so far from God that they can't be redeemed. And if someone behaves significantly badly, then we have the right to impose a temporary ban for their sake and the sake of the church.

We've had encounters when someone walked into the church saying he was looking for someone. He had a big raincoat on and revealed that he had sewn in large knives into the coat because he had come to kill someone. Machetes and bread knives. We've also had a member of the congregation leap over two rows and try to bite the nose off another member of the congregation, because he was going out with someone he went out with. We've had people having sex and taking drugs in the toilets. We have to say, 'We really like you, but we don't like what you're doing.' So, we must stop them coming for a while and withdraw them from services for a while. This means they cannot access the meals and community centres that come with the church community. It feels hard, but it's tough love. A ban can be for a week or two weeks. We've only imposed a long ban once. And they must come back with an apology. We thought that they would never come back, but they did.

One woman came to faith and gave up a heroin addiction, but her body was so knackered by the drugs that she died young at 48. Another man, who had come and wept because he wanted to be loved, died of a drugs overdose. Another person was murdered in the toilets for the sake of £5 that someone wanted for buying drugs. Even if the world crashes because they screwed up, they were still deserving of God's love. I don't tell these stories very often because you can wear them like badges and say, 'Look what we've done', and that doesn't honour the people to whom this happens. But we still work with people who hate themselves and who are asking 'How do I do this?' meaning, 'How do I live?'

If one takes the view that church is for all, and not just for the middle class or the well-educated, then faith is for all and social justice is for all. towards those in society who most people would prefer not to see or think they should all be in jail.

We have accompanied members of our congregation to magistrate's hearings and family courts about child custody. Social justice is for everyone, not just for those who can afford it or understand it. Our benefits system is terribly complicated and difficult to understand. At our community centre, which is our daughter organisation, we have a footfall of 33,000 a year. We provide support around health, money, debt, advice on rights and helping people to access the benefits they are entitled to.

We take Matthew 25:35–40 seriously – when did we see you thirsty? This is updated to: when did we help someone fill out a benefits form or accompany you to a magistrate's hearing? Through relationship we have earned the right to speak into people's lives and help them. We don't think of Matthew 25 as a command. It arises more organically.

Our compassion grew out of having our hearts broken because of what we saw. It caused us to have a desire to engage more intentionally with those who are in significant need. In other words, it encouraged us to get out more to meet people where they were.

Long gone are the days where people flocked to church. We need to be out and about, getting outside the church walls and meeting people where they are.

When we did this and started caring about the things that they care about and started building real relationships, that's when God started doing good, awesome stuff. The kind of stuff that only he can do. The kind of stuff that blows you away. Because our intentional relationship-building allowed us to authentically speak hope, self-worth and love into the lives of those who often feel like they have been forgotten or feel like they are unimportant, unwanted or have no voice.

Ignite

And that's where Ignite comes in. Ignite didn't start as a clever PCC strategy. Ignite is a Christian faith community, but it's got no strings attached. People choose how much or how little they buy into the whole Christianity idea. Our aim is to build a community that values and builds people up regardless of their level of faith, because we believe that offering community is profoundly important in and of itself. Good community supports and encourages and values. Good community breathes life into people. It doesn't suck life out of them.

Jesus said, 'If anyone is thirsty, let him come to me and drink' (see John 7:37–38). And so, if we are thinking about what it means to give drink to those who are thirsty, then I suppose you could say that in the middle of a challenging world, a largely unkind world, a world where many people are pushed aside or relegated to society's margins, then an Ignite community tries to be an oasis. It tries to be an oasis where people can have both their spiritual and physical thirst quenched in the most gentle and user-friendly way possible. We provide the opportunity for people to meet Jesus and to drink if they want to.

In addition to being a Christian faith community, Ignite also does something fundamentally important, because it recognises that we are all on this journey together.

It's a shared learning experience. As Christian practitioners, we're not just giving out answers. We are also learning from those who we engage with. We grapple with hard questions together. We don't always agree on the answers, but together we move deeper into our relationship with each other and more importantly, in our relationship with Jesus.

Refreshment and refuge

As guests arrive at an Ignite gathering, they are met and welcomed, and they're given a name label so that everyone can be addressed and known by name. It's such an innocuous little thing, but having our name known is a big deal to God. It's mentioned numerous times in scripture, 'I have redeemed you; I have called you by name; you are mine' (Isaiah 43:1). It reminds me of the theme tune for the 1980s American sitcom *Cheers*, which included a line about going to a place 'where everybody knows your name'. The show is particularly appropriate and poignant, because *Cheers* was based in a bar where people went to have a drink and to be with friends and to share their woes. Someone knowing your name is so powerful and affirming. It highlights that we are alive, that we have a place in this world and that we matter.

> Someone knowing your name is so powerful and affirming. It highlights that we are alive, that we have a place in this world and that we matter.

People have dared to come to Ignite thirsty for something they probably couldn't even articulate. They needed friendship, companionship, love. They needed a God who could give them all of that and much, much more. Dare I say that many of them are a bit like the Samaritan woman whom Jesus meets at the well; the woman who has been ostracised by her community because of the way that she has lived her life, particularly with men. She goes and gets water when there's nobody else there. She doesn't go at the popular times. She goes at the times maybe when the sun is at its hottest. She has lost her voice within the community. But in her engagement with Jesus, even though he's the one who initially asks her for a drink, she realises the depths of her own need for spiritual water. And Jesus is the drink that she needs. And suddenly, and I love this, she finds her voice. Suddenly she is vocally celebrating what she has discovered: 'Come quick. Come, and see a man who told me everything I ever did. Could this be the Messiah? Quick, come.'

Resonating out

She drank from living water and found a voice. And in the same way, but perhaps not such a dramatic way, many people coming to Ignite discover their voice of encouragement. At Ignite, faith permeates all that we do, and guests decide for themselves at what level they participate. They choose how much they want to drink, whether to just have a sip or to go all in like the Samaritan woman. They might just choose to dip in and out or simply enjoy our hospitality, and that's great; we want them to come. Or they might engage with the activities and the discussions, as a means of socialising or building themselves up, which is fantastic. Or they might choose to allow themselves to be open to an ever-present faith that exists within, to gradually lead them into a transformational encounter with our amazing and loving God.

Over the years many people who have come to Ignite have been baptised, and I've had the privilege of baptising many adults.

Coincidentally, St Paul's Church is the only Anglican church in the diocese where people can be baptised by full immersion. Many people recognise that there is something inherently powerful about not just having a drink, but being all in and under the water and coming up as a new creation.

There's a man from Ramsgate who said: 'It's not like church. It's not religious, more like a social club. But I have learned a lot about God.' I think this is high praise indeed. And it paints a beautiful picture of God's church that I absolutely love to bits. But I say, in all seriousness, I am a semi-competent screw-up who loves Jesus and who has discovered that I need to drink from him myself often.

What people who attend Ignite say about it

'It's just getting out and meeting people and having somewhere to go when times are crap!'

'Before I met Patrick and Debbie I was a horrible person – and I mean horrible! I met Patrick and Debbie and started coming to Ignite and it just changed me. I got my faith back, I was baptised, and now I work here as well. It changed me for the better.'

'It was really like coming across my faith for the first time. I would never have walked in here on a Sunday. It was the gentle way that Ignite brought me in, teaching me a few things, and about me asking, "Who are these crazy people and why do they care about me? I'd like to get to know them."'

'My faith has been challenged a lot over the past couple of years and I thought God had deserted me and left me. I come here and everyone sort of lifts me up. We have a chat and a pray, and I feel lifted. It puts everything back into perspective. It's a good thing.'

'It is really good fun and it's good to see people coming in and rid of their problems for a little while and learning how better to deal with their problems, because they have people who care and listen and help them and don't judge them.'

'It's about meeting people where they are, wherever it may be, in their brokenness, in their sense of being lost, and trying to find them and help them find a way to make sense of this crazy world we live in.'

 ## Reflection

- Where do you find relationships, resonance and refuge?
- Who in your community needs your friendship? Do you know their name?
- What does God have to say to you about the living water of Christ?
- What is Christ saying to you at Jacob's well?

 ## A prayer

O God, who breathed over the waters to create life, pour into our hearts your refreshing, saving gift of eternal love. Help us, we pray, to share the resources of our planet with all those who are thirsty for refreshment and relationship – with you and with one another. May those who thirst be satisfied in body and soul. We pray in the name of Jesus Christ, the living water. Amen.

 ## A spiritual exercise

Prepare yourself for prayer
Sit comfortably with both feet on the ground and hands open on your lap as if waiting to receive a gift from God. Let go of your worries or

thoughts and entrust yourself and everything to God. Pray that you will be receptive to what God has to say to you in this scripture reading.

Read the passage below out loud, slowly and meditatively. Listen for words or phrases that speak to you. Sit with it for a while.

> While they were eating, Jesus took a loaf of bread, and after blessing it he broke it, gave it to the disciples, and said, 'Take, eat; this is my body.' Then he took a cup, and after giving thanks he gave it to them, saying, 'Drink from it, all of you, for this is my blood of the covenant, which is poured out for many for the forgiveness of sins. I tell you, I will never again drink of this fruit of the vine until that day when I drink it new with you in my Father's kingdom.'
> When they had sung the hymn, they went out to the Mount of Olives.
>
> MATTHEW 26:26–30

Meditate
Read these verses again. This time, let the words or phrases that stood out for you the first time become an invitation from God to speak with him. Allow the words to flow through you as you meditate upon them.

Pray
Now read the passage a third time, slowly.

Ask
- What is God saying to you in these words?
- What do you want to say to God?
- What feelings are stirred within you?
- Share your answers with God.

Contemplate
Read the text one last time, and this time let the words you have been praying with go free. Be still and at peace with God.

Ask
- What gift has God given you to take away?
- What action might God be inviting you to undertake?
- Thank God for this gift and for his invitation.

Further resources

Allison Allen, *Thirsty for More: Discovering God's unexpected blessings in a desert season* (Revell, 2018).

'"A more relaxed environment" – Estates Churches: St Paul's Cliftonville, Margate', YouTube video, **youtube.com/watch?v=X1Bfaqp8YOg**.

Patrick and Debbie Ellisdon, *Ignite* (BRF, forthcoming 2025).

Hannah Hall, *Thirsty: 12 weeks of drinking deeply from God's word* (Revell, 2022).

Ignite, **canterburydiocese.org/mission/ignite**

Mez McConnell, *The Least, the Last and the Lost: Understanding poverty in the UK and the responsibility of the local church* (Evangelical Press, 2021).

Henri J. M. Nouwen, *Can You Drink the Cup?* (Ave Maria Press, 2006).

Ghislaine Howard
The Return of the Prodigal Son
2014
Acrylic on canvas
244 x 183 cm

Ghislaine Howard
Seven Acts of Mercy: Bury the Dead
2020
Acrylic on canvas
102 x 127 cm

Ghislaine Howard
Seven Acts of Mercy: Feed the Hungry
2013
Oil and pigment on flax
102 x 127 cm

Ghislaine Howard
Seven Acts of Mercy: Visit the Sick
2004
Acrylic on canvas
102 x 127 cm

6

SONGS IN THE KEY OF LIFE: FINDING HOME

'I was naked and you gave me clothing.'
MATTHEW 25:36

If any of your kin fall into difficulty and become dependent on you, you shall support them; they shall live with you as though resident aliens. Do not take interest in advance or otherwise make a profit from them, but fear your God; let them live with you. You shall not lend them your money at interest taken in advance or provide them food at a profit. I am the Lord your God who brought you out of the land of Egypt, to give you the land of Canaan, to be your God.
LEVITICUS 25:35–38

An expert in the law stood up to test Jesus. 'Teacher,' he said, 'what must I do to inherit eternal life?' He said to him, 'What is written in the law? What do you read there?' He answered, 'You shall love the Lord your God with all your heart and with all your soul and with all your strength and with all your mind and your neighbour as yourself.' And he said to him, 'You have given the right answer; do this, and you will live.'

But wanting to vindicate himself, he asked Jesus, 'And who is my neighbour?' Jesus replied, 'A man was going down from

Jerusalem to Jericho and fell into the hands of robbers, who stripped him, beat him, and took off, leaving him half dead. Now by chance a priest was going down that road, and when he saw him he passed by on the other side. So likewise a Levite, when he came to the place and saw him, passed by on the other side. But a Samaritan while travelling came upon him, and when he saw him he was moved with compassion. He went to him and bandaged his wounds, treating them with oil and wine. Then he put him on his own animal, brought him to an inn, and took care of him. The next day he took out two denarii, gave them to the innkeeper, and said, "Take care of him, and when I come back I will repay you whatever more you spend." Which of these three, do you think, was a neighbour to the man who fell into the hands of the robbers?' He said, 'The one who showed him mercy.' Jesus said to him, 'Go and do likewise.'

LUKE 10:25–37

Much of what Jesus says about encountering others in Matthew 25:35–40 relates to those who are the least provided and cared for in our society: the hungry, the thirsty, those who are cold from lack of clothing or shelter, those who get sick because they must live on our streets. This chapter is devoted to encountering the homeless because it underpins so many of the works of mercy.

In music we use the terminology of 'home' and 'key' to help navigate where we are in the music. A 'home key' is often the musical key in which a piece starts and finishes. If a piece of music is in the key of C major, we expect that it will begin using melodies and harmonies that are in tune with the tones and semitones of C major (all the white keys on a piano keyboard). The piece may then meander to other keys, such as its 'relative' A minor, or modulate to another key, or a variety of keys, through variations and developments as the composer or songwriter sees fit. But often, the piece will find its way back home to C major. It will cadence back to where it started. It returns home.

Unlike the interrupted cadence, which leaves the music and the listener stranded in an alien sound world, which can be unresolved, unsatisfying and disturbing, the return to the home key feels like a resolution, a return to safety.

In 1975, the great R&B and pop singer Stevie Wonder considered leaving the music industry, at the height of his musical powers. He wanted to emigrate to Ghana to work with disabled children, motivated by his anger with the US government. He changed his mind, however, and instead recorded one of the greatest albums in pop history, *Songs in the Key of Life*, released in 1976. As the title suggests, the tracks reflect Wonder's key life experiences, with different seasons, memories, encounters and loves – its keys.

Those who are made homeless, for whatever reason, have often had their lives disrupted by life events, whether that be abuse, family breakdown, addiction, bereavement, losing a job or some other misfortune or mistake. Finding one's way 'home' can be a difficult task, especially if home is no longer a safe place of sanctuary or when home no longer exists. In such circumstances the question is, 'Where can I find home?' So, I would like to begin with a question. Where is home for you?

A place to call home

Where is home for you? Is it where you live now? Is it the place where you were born or grew up? Is it the place in which you no longer live, but is still home in your heart? Is it a place that you have left temporarily to come and live somewhere else?

There are few things quite as important as a sense of home. Somewhere we feel at rest, where we can be ourselves. For some, that place may be somewhere that is yet to be found or has been, for whatever reason, lost. Like the Son of Man, many on our streets have nowhere to lay their head. So how do we reconcile the disparity between the housed and the homeless? And how do the two encounter each other?

In this chapter we will hear stories that reveal the complexities involved in homelessness and with our engagement with those who have no homes. The fact is that the problems are complicated and when we multiply these stories by the number of homeless people, we may get a sense of hopelessness ourselves. The number of homeless in the UK has been rising year on year, and with the cost-of-living crisis, it looks set to continue rising. Behind each case there may be a narrative of family problems, addiction, debt or other factors. And beyond our shores there are millions more being displaced from their homes by war, oppression or climate change.

The task is great and going to become greater, so we must not give up on mercy. If we do, we not only give up on our faith in humanity to do good, we not only dehumanise others, but we also fail something divine within us. In his book entitled *In God's Hands*, which was commissioned by the Archbishop of Canterbury for Lent, Desmond Tutu stated that the Bible is:

> **The task is great and going to become greater, so we must not give up on mercy.**

> more revolutionary, more subversive of injustice and oppression than any political manifesto or ideology. How so? The Bible asserts… that each one of us, without exception, is created in the image of God. Whether you are rich or poor, white or black, educated or illiterate, male or female – each one of us, exhilaratingly, wonderfully, is created in the image of God.

This, says Tutu, makes each one of us a 'God-carrier'. He goes on:

> If we really believe this assertion, then we would be appalled at any ill-treatment of another human being, because it is not simply unjust but also, shockingly, blasphemous. It is really like spitting in the face of God.[55]

This is why the book of Leviticus demands that if someone is homeless, displaced and in need, they should be supported by the Israelites, remembering that God brought them out of the land of Egypt and home to the land of Canaan. And when the lawyer, in Luke's gospel, asks, 'Who is my neighbour?', Jesus replies with the story of the good Samaritan. The priest and the Levite pass by the wounded and abandoned man, but it is the Samaritan, traditionally an enemy of the Jews, who bandaged the victim's wounds, soothed them with wine and oil, placed him on his own animal to carry him to an inn, and gave the innkeeper the promise of additional money to care for the man until he was well. Who was this man's neighbour, Christ asks the lawyer: the one who truly encountered him as another human being, a fellow 'God-carrier', and showed him mercy.

Here are some more tales of encounter. First, from Jo, who is a chaplain to the homeless and parish priest, and then Kelly, who is our support manager for the project called 'Break the Cycle', which houses prison leavers who would otherwise be street homeless, and who wish to break the cycle of reoffending and addiction.

JO'S STORY

'Homeless chaplaincy and social justice really put fire in my belly. I have a passion for it', says Jo, a town-centre priest. For Jo, everyone who is homeless in Canterbury is a parishioner just like everyone else. She often does a prayer walk on a Monday through the city and makes a point of stopping and chatting. She works with Catching Lives, a local homeless charity, and she likes to go round the streets at six in the morning, because at that time 'you know who is genuinely on the streets'. With those who sleep rough in St Mildred's Church, Jo is 'firm but compassionate', but also tries to 'see the face of Jesus in the other'. The reasons for homelessness are many. 'One story I heard was of a guy who was on £3,000 a month with a car, a house and a job. He had everything. He was a commuter up to London. But his relationship broke down, which led to a spiral downwards.'

Jo takes inspiration from the Bible and particularly from those stories where Jesus encounters someone in need: 'Years ago a Franciscan nun told me that she'd just led a quiet day on one of Jesus' encounters – the man by the pool (John 5:1–18) – and as she told me this I had a powerful experience of the Holy Spirit. I was shaking and crying. Afterwards I asked myself, "What was pertinent about that story?" "Is it a message to me? Get yourself up and move." Also, the story of Jesus on the road to Emmaus Road (Luke 24:13–35) keeps me motivated. It's about walking with people, being non-judgemental, nurturing any faith that they have, but waiting for their invitation into their lives.'

'Is that mission or evangelism?' Jo asks. Her answer is that it is 'the evangelism of relationship-building. It's just about meeting people where they are, of all faiths and none.' Jo emphasises the incarnational aspect of ministry: 'Someone asked me, "Why don't you invite the homeless into church?" Well, I do, but I also take church out to them.'

Although most homeless people wish to be housed, not everybody wants accommodation. Sometimes we can try to be a saviour for others and find solutions to what we think is their problem. But is that our agenda or their agenda? 'Two people I know,' Jo says, 'John and Buffy, lived homeless for 18 years. Only two years ago did they want to be accommodated. Living with claustrophobia, John didn't want a small room on his own. John was the "Father of the Street" for many years. But he said, "I had to be ready to go inside." He did it gradually, starting with one night a week, then two. Mental health is a huge issue, and it can be a barrier to accommodation.'

Patient travelling

True encounter, then, can be about patient travelling with someone over a long period of time. And on that patient journey with those we encounter, we see God's work. Jo has more prayer requests from the homeless community than from anyone else in her parishes, and they often pray for her as well as with her. 'This is not a "rich" person's white Messiah complex, about those who "have" faith going out to give it to those who "don't". Spirituality on the streets is profound. Sacramentality and blessing are found on our streets. Who receives the blessing from this ministry? I've knelt and received a blessing from them, and I bless them if asked.'

Sadly, Jo also encounters grief and tragic death: 'Baz, who used to live in the churchyard at St Peter's, died this year of cancer,' Jo relates. 'His family wanted his funeral in St Peter's, so we had a full funeral with many of the homeless community present. They left their beer at the door and were hugely reverent and respectful. We recently had a memorial service for those who died on the streets in recent years. We had 86 names to be remembered and about 40 homeless people present in the congregation. They sometimes lose a friend, and they don't have closure, so there are huge amounts of raw emotion.'

Recognising another's dignity is also an important factor in encounter and building trust. The gospel story of Jesus casting out demons into the swine (Mark 5:1–20) is special to Jo for this reason: 'Jesus dignified the man by recognising his humanity and by asking his name. I always ask people their names, sit down with them (don't tower over them), and give them time. It has taken a long time to get there, but now they know where to find me and I know where to find them.'

Meaningful encounter with another takes time, trust and intention.

Jo's story reveals how meaningful encounter with another takes time, trust and intention. It requires us to be patient, to journey alongside, to recognise the God-given dignity of the other, to build relationship and not judge. And to be open to, and expect, that the mercy we receive from the poor may be of more lasting value than the financial or practical help we can offer them. We do not need to pretend that they are Christ when we can genuinely see the face of Christ and the work of God in them.

 **Reflection**

- Where do you encounter homelessness in your community?
- Are you patiently travelling with anyone now?
- When has your life been interrupted or disrupted?
- When do you feel most at home?

KELLY'S STORY

Kelly's motivation for this work was born out of her own experience: 'I was homeless with my three kids in Swanage in Dorset. Not street homeless but bandied about. At one point I was living in a caravan. I advocated for myself and campaigned for my own rights. Then I discovered others who didn't advocate for themselves and didn't know their rights.' So, Kelly saw both a social problem and an opportunity. She is articulate and feisty enough to fight for her rights. But she noticed those around her who did not have the skill, or the nerve, to do so, and she could help.

'I joined Citizen's Advice Bureau (CAB)', says Kelly, 'and trained as a CAB advisor in the evenings, while my kids were asleep. I had a particular interest in social policy. I was a generalist advisor at Wareham in Purbeck. Then I moved to Canterbury and became a service manager at Folkestone CAB and wrote up the social policy and housing reports.'

Kelly's vision and hard work were leading her down a path that would help thousands over the years, but then family tragedy struck as her son, Louis, was diagnosed with a brain tumour, meaning she had to take redundancy. Nevertheless, while caring for Louis, she continued and worked at winter night shelters. Louis was ill for six long years, but Kelly retained her passion to help the disadvantaged.

'I was invited to volunteer for the homeless charity Catching Lives,' Kelly relates. 'We developed Campaign Kent because there was zero government funding or priority given to people who came out of prison into homelessness. I took social policy reporting to Catching Lives and called it "Evidence and Impact Statements", because anecdotes are fine but you need evidence.' Kelly would talk to people who had experienced social injustice, write it up as a case file, code it and then see how many other cases presented the same problem, thus creating a body of evidence. 'Social policy is not just pointing the finger of blame,' Kelly says. 'It is solution focused.'

One of many reports collected by Kelly and Campaign Kent as they analysed true stories of homelessness is the story of Sam (not his real name), who was released from prison into homelessness. Sam had been street homeless since the age of 16 due to a relationship breakdown with his parents. He has been involved in drugs since this time, mainly cocaine and amphetamines, then later heroin. His criminal activity, with over 50 convictions, was drug-related. Kelly's report relates that, 'When put before every judge, at no time did anyone suggest that Sam needed rehabilitation rather than prison. It seemed that the reason for his criminal activity was ignored.'

After his last sentence Sam was released from prison and given £46 and a travel warrant to Margate, the very place where he had been lost in addiction. The prison resettlement team apparently released Sam to street homelessness knowing that he had a history of repeat offending, substance misuse and mental health issues.

Kelly concludes her report with this summary: 'Sam feels like nothing has changed since his last sentence, and that every time is the same, apart from his motivation to get clean while inside this time. He feels it won't be long before he is back in prison for another drug-related crime. He is surrounded by the people he used drugs with and feels that he won't stop using unless this changes. Sam feels frustrated and fed up with the cyclical behaviour he feels trapped in. He stated that he needs support. Sam has been estranged from his parents since the age of 16, and he said that he would want to reconnect with his parents, but only when he feels they can be proud of him. He stated that all he wants is a job and somewhere to live which is out of the area so he can start afresh.'

Kelly's compassion and action for people like Sam arise out of her own trauma. 'I have a good therapist! I had a massive crash after Louis got well. I had four years of being completely lost and of not knowing where to go, what to do or how to work, but I tried to keep collecting data. The campaign work was a kind of escape. Being able to research my own situation and fight my own battles when I needed to, helped me to fight for other people.'

Kelly's empirical approach not only brings to light the number of cases that have similar patterns or characteristics, but also the case files can be used to lobby government and councils and provide evidence to non-government organisations of precisely what kind of provision is needed. The empirical approach also helps those in need. For example, Kelly enjoys encouraging people by measuring their progress in numbers: 'Because I use empirical data, I can say to someone, "Your mental health score was 42 the other day and it's 55 today, which tells me you're feeling better; that's a great achievement." I count everything, write everything down and map trends. I anonymise the case records so that The Probation Service can look at them.' But the empiricism is matched by enthusiasm: 'I have always been passionate about homelessness,' Kelly says. 'I understand the impact of trauma and what it's like not to have a home, and people's nonchalant attitude to you when you are in that situation. You need to be heard. I didn't recognise my own trauma for some time. But seeing it on paper I realised, and it helps me help others. It's a huge factor in how I work with people who made poor choices.'

Kelly doesn't back away from the fact that often people's difficulties have arisen from poor choices. But the difference between Kelly and many other people is that she doesn't dismiss anyone as beyond help because they contributed to their own distress, or say, 'They only have themselves to blame.' Common examples of poor choices are substance abuse and crime, and they are often related.

'People ask, "What came first, the drugs or the crime?" That's the classic chicken-and-egg situation,' Kelly says. 'Usually it's a drug first, but the drugs are the self-medication trying to put a plaster over the trauma. Our project, and my job, is to rip the plaster off. Because unless you do, what is going to change?'

Like Jo, Kelly recognises that to make any difference you must respect another's dignity and be ready to stay with them on a journey that may be painful and take time but will build trust. 'I do the work not because of my experience but because of the people I have met. When I helped people at the night shelters, it was heart-rending because these people could have been "saved" a long time ago, although I don't like that word. I am not a saviour. My reward is helping someone to achieve what they can at the time that they need to achieve it. It's little things, like having someone say, "I hate volunteering," but then they end up doing it two days a week quite happily.'

Kelly's story is an encouragement that, even when living without a permanent home, trying to raise children and dealing with a serious illness, she found it possible to work, train and fight for her own rights and for the rights of others. When combined with a fiery passion for justice, results are amazingly widespread and lasting. Kelly's encounter with her own poverty and trauma has led to countless encounters where lives have been transformed.

So where is home for you? Well, wherever it is, or will be, in this life, it is inevitably temporary. As God-carriers we may not be able to solve all hunger, thirst, sickness, nakedness, imprisonment or homelessness. But we can, if we are brave, show mercy to those in need in the way we live our lives, spend our money and use our time. We can recognise the divine spark in each other that deserves our respect and honour, our care and our love.

 ## Reflection

- How has Kelly's life experience shaped her passions today?
- How have your life experiences shaped your life?
- How might you walk alongside those who are displaced from their homes?

 ## A prayer

Loving God, you call each of us by name as your beloved children. In this transitory life, with so many changes and disruptions, may we help the displaced and the lost to find rest and safety, until we, with them, find our eternal homes in your kingdom of mercy and justice. Amen.

 ## A spiritual exercise

Prepare yourself for prayer
Sit comfortably with both feet on the ground and hands open on your lap as if waiting to receive a gift from God. Let go of your worries or

thoughts and entrust yourself and everything to God. Pray that you will be receptive to what God has to say to you in this scripture reading.

Read the passage below out loud, slowly and meditatively. Listen for words or phrases that speak to you. Sit with it for a while.

Now on that same day two of them were going to a village called Emmaus, about seven miles from Jerusalem, and talking with each other about all these things that had happened. While they were talking and discussing, Jesus himself came near and went with them, but their eyes were kept from recognising him. And he said to them, 'What are you discussing with each other while you walk along?' They stood still, looking sad. Then one of them, whose name was Cleopas, answered him, 'Are you the only stranger in Jerusalem who does not know the things that have taken place there in these days?' He asked them, 'What things?' They replied, 'The things about Jesus of Nazareth, who was a prophet mighty in deed and word before God and all the people, and how our chief priests and leaders handed him over to be condemned to death and crucified him. But we had hoped that he was the one to redeem Israel. Yes, and besides all this, it is now the third day since these things took place. Moreover, some women of our group astounded us. They were at the tomb early this morning, and when they did not find his body there they came back and told us that they had indeed seen a vision of angels who said that he was alive. Some of those who were with us went to the tomb and found it just as the women had said, but they did not see him.' Then he said to them, 'Oh, how foolish you are and how slow of heart to believe all that the prophets have declared! Was it not necessary that the Messiah should suffer these things and then enter into his glory?' Then beginning with Moses and all the prophets, he interpreted to them the things about himself in all the scriptures.
As they came near the village to which they were going, he walked ahead as if he were going on. But they urged him strongly, saying, 'Stay with us, because it is almost evening and the day is

now nearly over.' So he went in to stay with them. When he was at the table with them, he took bread, blessed and broke it, and gave it to them. Then their eyes were opened, and they recognised him, and he vanished from their sight. They said to each other, 'Were not our hearts burning within us while he was talking to us on the road, while he was opening the scriptures to us?' That same hour they got up and returned to Jerusalem, and they found the eleven and their companions gathered together. They were saying, 'The Lord has risen indeed, and he has appeared to Simon!' Then they told what had happened on the road and how he had been made known to them in the breaking of the bread.

LUKE 24:13–35

Meditate

Read these verses again. This time, let the words or phrases that stood out for you the first time become an invitation from God to speak with him. Allow the words to flow through you as you meditate upon them.

Pray

Now read the passage a third time, slowly.

Ask

- What is God saying to you in these words?
- What do you want to say to God?
- What feelings are stirred within you?
- Share your answers with God.

Contemplate

Read the text one last time, and this time let the words you have been praying with go free. Be still and at peace with God.

Ask

- What gift has God given you to take away?
- To what action might God be inviting you?
- Thank God for this gift and for his invitation.

Further resources

Marjorie Bard, *Shadow Women: Homeless women's survival stories* (Rowman and Littlefield, 1990).

The Benefice of St Dunstan's Church, St Mildred's Church and St Peter's Church in Canterbury, **dunstanmildredpeter.org.uk/welcome.htm**

Break The Cycle, **canterburydiocese.org/mission/together-kent/break-the-cycle**

Catching Lives, **catchinglives.org**

Citizens Advice, **citizensadvice.org.uk**

The Connexion: Doing justice (Methodist Publishing, 2022).

Crisis, 'Get help if you're experiencing homelessness', **crisis.org.uk/get-help/how-to-get-help**

The Commission of the Archbishops of Canterbury and York on Housing, Church and Community, *Coming Home: Tackling the housing crisis together* (Church House, 2021), **churchofengland.org/about/archbishops-commissions/housing-church-and-community/about-coming-home**

James F. Keenan and Mark McGreevy (eds), *Street Homelessness and Catholic Theological Ethics* (Orbis Books, 2019).

Roger Quick, *Sheltering Saints: Living with the homeless* (Darton, Longman and Todd, 2022).

UK Government, 'Help if you're homeless or about to become homeless', **gov.uk/if-youre-homeless-at-risk-of-homelessness**

Ed Walker, *A House Built on Love: The enterprising team creating homes for the homeless* (SPCK, 2020).

7

'HOW CAN WE SING THE LORD'S SONG IN A STRANGE LAND?': WELCOMING THE STRANGER

'I was a stranger and you welcomed me.'
MATTHEW 25:35

By the rivers of Babylon –
   there we sat down, and there we wept
   when we remembered Zion.
On the willows there
   we hung up our harps.
For there our captors
   asked us for songs,
and our tormentors asked for mirth, saying,
   'Sing us one of the songs of Zion!'
How could we sing the Lord's song
   in a foreign land?
PSALM 137:1–4

When an alien resides with you in your land, you shall not oppress the alien. The alien who resides with you shall be to you as the native-born among you; you shall love the alien as yourself, for you were aliens in the land of Egypt: I am the Lord your God.
LEVITICUS 19:33–34

Rafiq looks at me with tears in his eyes. He has just arrived from Syria. His hometown and his country have been shattered by invasion and bombing. He has fled with his wife Halimah and their children, to begin a new life. We struggle to communicate in English and Arabic, but it is clear this is a family devastated by circumstance. With pride they introduce their three boys, but the memory and current reality of this transition is heavy upon them. 'We have lost everything. We don't know what to do,' he says. They are heartbroken to leave their home and country behind. They have been welcomed into a new home, and are being helped to settle into new work, schools and communities. There are people to stand alongside them, to walk with them through the coming months and years. But now there is trauma and sadness in the eyes of Rafiq, whose name in Arabic means 'friend'. Halimah means 'gentle patience'. They will need friendship and patience in the time ahead.

This encounter happened in a museum in Canterbury, while we were celebrating a project called 'Home' with Syrian refugees, developed and run by Domenica, our refugee projects manager. The room was full of fabric, paints, needlework, pictures and wall hangings, all of which were the result of a collaboration with an artist. Children and adults jostled together in the small space as we marvelled at the joy this project brought. The atmosphere somehow seemed to hold the grief of Rafiq, Halimah and their family. Their tragedy formed a kind of lens through which we saw everyone there. But there was also hope, friendship and gentle patience.

I felt a stranger myself in Canterbury, in a very small way, but I too was welcomed, and in turn found myself welcoming the stranger. In these people, who had lost everything, I could see God, both in the present and in the centuries of migration in human history in which people have fled from oppression and violence. God was in this moment, as he is in every moment.

Being with Rafiq and Halimah reminded me of Psalm 137. Written at a time of exile, the Jewish people had been invaded and forced into captivity in Babylon. They wept when they remembered their homeland. In their insensitivity, the Babylonians wanted the Israelites to sing to them songs of their homeland. 'Sing us one of the songs of Zion!' (v. 3). But how could they? They had hung up their harps in despair and grief. How could they sing the Lord's song in a strange land? What place could music have in such desolation?

In East Kent we not only work with refugees from Afghanistan, Syria and Ukraine, but we are on the front line of receiving asylum seekers arriving in small boats on the south coast. This makes Canterbury a unique diocese in the Church of England and sets us some serious challenges as well as opportunities. For those who have fled oppression, war or the results of climate change, seeking asylum can be a terrifying and bewildering process. For those who are granted asylum, one way in which we can ease the transition is by helping people to find their voice, whether through language classes or listening to their story and what they can contribute to our communities. Through mutual exchange of culture, knowledge and intertwining melodies of friendship, we have found how we can talk to and understand one another, and even to sing together. Encountering new cultures, songs and stories, strengthens the orchestra of our society, with new instruments incorporated and new tunes to learn. Every voice heard and listened to adds to the polyphonic texture of our communities.

Through mutual exchange of culture, knowledge and friendship, we can talk to and understand one another.

Here are some stories about how people in East Kent and in Calais have responded to the needs of those who have fled war, oppression, famine and injustice.

DOMENICA'S STORY

My role involves reaching out to our church, civic society and refugee communities to address the needs of those who have been forcibly displaced. Our aim is to open people's hearts and minds to the plight of refugees and to the challenges and beauty of welcoming the stranger as valued members and neighbours of the community.

In April 2022, we set up the first Welcome Hub in Kent for newly arrived Ukrainian families and UK sponsors. The Hub operates as a weekly drop-in. We organise workshops on how the system works in the UK regarding housing, community safety, education, universal credit, budgeting and so on.

A separate venture, The Welcome Cafe, supports refugees and people seeking sanctuary living in the Canterbury area. The project provides accessible English classes and employment support to people with personal experience of forced displacement.

Language barriers and unfamiliarity with the new environment trap new arrivals in a spiral of unemployment and diminishes their ability to feel part of the fabric of the new society. Becoming fluent in English and finding work are interlinked indicators of social integration. However, we provide extra value by developing a sense of belonging to the local community. For example, a key feature of our format is sharing a main meal with local volunteers as part of the activities. These rituals have become significant for people and help level out power dynamics so often overlooked in service delivery. We want to help people regain their dignity while at the same time helping our local community to grow in solidarity with those less fortunate.

For Afghan families we run a 'one-stop shop welcome'. This is a weekly drop-in service offering informal English classes for Afghan women. We distribute essential items in collaboration with local charities and the local mosque.

For schools, we run the Voices of Welcome as a part of our School of Sanctuary work, aimed at fostering a welcoming school community through participatory workshops with children coming from different life trajectories.

We also lead an online conversation club for refugee women, and I am also leading the setting up of a multifaith prayer room in Manston Detention Centre, where asylum seekers are held and processed. For Refugee Week 2023, we organised a series of events focusing on the trap that modern slavery may present to people. We cannot do this without volunteers, who are pivotal to the running and to the success of the projects. We also have a Ukrainian 'Homes for Ukraine' support worker.

My national work is focused on the growth of the resettlement scheme through community sponsorship, which is a community-led, government-overseen scheme that aims to bring to safety families who are in refugee camps across the world. The United Nations High Commissioner for Refugees has the remit of identifying refugees and informing the Home Office of the need for resettlement. The scheme is run by community groups who want to sponsor a family, to bring the family to the UK and work towards their independence. This kind of work is slow and it's important not to be discouraged by how much time it takes to achieve the outcome you want. We are now working with Reset to draft a community sponsorship strategy for the Church of England.

Internationally we are part of an organisation set up by the Church of Sweden called World of Neighbours, which is like an international support group, where we share what is on our hearts and we have an opportunity to learn a broader understanding of how refugee work is done.

Challenges

One of the biggest challenges is to address where people are fearful and to help to promote, to the church and the wider society, an understanding of the realities of asylum seeking, why we should be involved with it and what people can do to open their hearts and minds.

On the one hand, for those who want to volunteer, we can provide tools for them to offer voluntary help that is within their comfort zone. For the more adventurous we can provide tools for those who want to be pushed outside of their comfort zone. People question why we should welcome asylum seekers. But would we question their right to seek asylum here if they were wealthy? Sometimes the issue with refugees is pretty much interlinked with how we welcome the poor. I can decide what is the best place and the best circumstances to bring up my family, so why should other people not have the same freedom?

Then there are refugees in northern France, for example, in the Calais area. They have gone through in an unimaginable situation in their own countries. They hope to cross and start a new life here. To take the risk of travelling across the channel in a small boat, knowing that for some of them it could be disastrous – why would people do that? A popular answer is that they speak English and have been given the impression that the UK is the place where their family will flourish. Indeed, some asylum seekers have been sold lies about what the UK can provide. One migrant was sitting on a bench in Manston Detention Centre, cold, wet and hungry, and said to the guard, 'When do I get the keys to my new house?' People are being told fairy tales. Smugglers and traffickers who organise the crossings are vicious, because they reinforce false hopes. Asylum seekers coming from war zones have lost relatives, friends, homes and jobs; they have lost their identity, their position within the family and the community. They have nothing more to lose. Refugees arrive without shoes, water or food, coupled with being brainwashed by criminal gangs who take their money for the crossing, creating a spiral of exploitation. It's very sad.

My motivation

I always wanted to work with those who were stigmatised, because they were thought to be hopeless. In my previous role working for a Muslim organisation, I happened to meet some women who were seeking asylum on the basis of domestic violence, which was when I realised I wanted to work with refugees. I was the only non-Muslim in the organisation. I saw all my colleagues praying three times during the working day, and having a direct relationship with God. It's very strange, but I really experienced Jesus in the eyes of so many Muslim kids. I have a spiritual foundation to do this work, which helps me not only personally but also professionally. There is an integrity that you need to carry out this work. What matters is the integrity you carry within yourself as you carry out your work.

 Reflection

- How does Domenica's work make you feel?
- If we welcome the stranger, we welcome Christ. How might this biblical truth affect our view of refugees and asylum seekers?
- When have you felt welcome somewhere or by someone else?

CHRIS' STORY

Romney Marsh is an area of enormous social deprivation. Local authorities dump people here into social housing, so I have a great interest in social justice. We set up a food bank four years ago. It's a weekly initiative but if people need food, we'll try to make sure they can access it or have it delivered anytime. We supplement this with pantries, ideas of how to cook and manage budgets, etc. Very few recipients come to church. People in a very poor area are incredibly generous. Most families who come to the food bank feel embarrassed and awkward about having to use it, so we try to minimise that and make sure people keep their dignity. We don't have much homelessness, which is more of an urban problem, but rural and farming problems are there and are less easy to address because they are often hidden.

Migrants arrive on the coastline of the Marsh, partly due to tides but also because the Dungeness power station is such a visible landmark. Migrants have been arriving here for a long time, often on very dangerous boats. The Dungeness lifeboats go out and save them. Some people see this as a 'taxi service' for refugees. Since Easter 2022 there has been a military presence and patrol (ship and helicopter patrols), but the lifeboat crews still go out. Sometimes the refugees go straight to Dover, where they are dealt with by Border Force or Interforce, but they often land on the beach here. We have a way of contacting a group of local people who can go to the beach to offer blankets, hot drinks, shoes, towels or anything else we can help with. Migrants often arrive soaking wet.

Attitudes have changed recently. Government agencies used to be wary of us, but now we are often asked to go and offer practical support. One lifeboat will bring around 45 people on to the beach, using a ladder to help people to come down. Three or four of us will greet them. There are practical ways we can support before they get on a bus about an hour later, which takes them to the processing centre.

Few are able to speak English, although some will have some words. Most will be happy to be there. Some get to their knees and pray. We give out blankets, biscuits, water and footwear so they can walk on the beach. The response is usually positive and grateful. Crossing the channel is terrifying. Some are distressed but mostly relieved. I was shocked recently to see a mother with a ten-day-old child. They have determination. Apparently one person is allocated to steer the boat and they get their passage for free.

We get contact from the far right about who is a worthy migrant, but I don't get into that debate. We help people who are cold and hungry and that's it. There is some far-right verbal abuse on the beach itself, but it is mainly online. Sometimes far-right groups will film them on the beach or wait to talk to the migrants and challenge them. We often give biscuits and water to the far right as well. We don't take sides.

The team of helpers are from the wider community. Three come from the church, but most are motivated by humanitarian principles. Care4Calais is the umbrella organisation who organises it.

I feel underpinned by Matthew 25:35–40: 'Where were you?' 'I was on the beach. I was giving out food.' Migrants are well documented in the Bible. We should be compassionate and caring for those who are seeking new homes. When I look at what I do and the opposition we face, I hold it up against biblical guidance, which seems to say firmly that what we are doing is unquestionably the

When I look at what I do and the opposition we face, I hold it up against biblical guidance.

right thing to do and in my ministry is the most important thing that I do.

I've only been ordained for ten years. I was a pub landlord for 30 years. I got to know people's characters well. It was a robust lifestyle. I came to ministry very reluctantly. It wasn't a Damascus moment. I had a brain tumour that required some intense surgery. Some people in the pub got a bit anxious about it. Before the operation I thought I would go to church, just in case, as a kind of investment!

There are similarities between churches and pubs, in that both provide regular engagement with people in the community to keep them coming back. Pubs are not governed by a parochial council, of course. But a pub does have a sense of mission in that you journey with people. There's always something going on and moving, which keeps the momentum going and people coming back. A landlord is a listening ear. When I was ordained, *The Sun* newspaper had the headline 'Ale Mary!', whereas the *Kentish Gazette* came out with 'From Last Orders to Holy Orders', which I thought was quite good.

Matthew 25:35–40 is a good yardstick by which to measure your performance. In the cold light of day, the question is 'Where were you?' It's a direct question that we will all be asked. It's part of the faith deal. And without faith I would struggle to do this. From a secular point of view there would be a feel-good element to doing this work, but it would be less fulfilling for me. As Christians, we examine ourselves and find ourselves wanting. We fall short with what we do for the migrants, but it's a step in the right direction. Migrants are on my doorstep, so this is one thing that I can do. And it's expensive in terms of time and money. It is demanding in terms of doing what is right, when so many people are telling you that it is wrong. So, there's no immediate reward from the community. There is opposition, and there is no publicity. I don't often mention it, and I don't preach about it. There's an element of sacrifice that isn't acknowledged by any public acclaim. The migrants themselves disappear, and I never see them again. It is fleeting. I get more out of that fleeting moment with a mother and child and helping them up the beach than I would from any public thanks. You know that you have briefly done something that helps someone in need.

— — — — — — — — — — — —

 Reflection

- What does a warm welcome look and sound like?
- What could you do to welcome a stranger?
- Does being a Christian make a difference to the action?
- Will we be judged on our efforts to fulfil the works of mercy?

Of course, not everyone shares these views or feelings about refugees and asylum seekers, especially in Kent, and it's important to have alternative viewpoints. David, at the port of Dover, helps us to see another side of the story.

DAVID'S STORY

— — — — — — — — — — — —

Having to move from home is truly biblical, starting with Adam and Eve, followed by Cain, then Abraham, Jacob, Joseph and the whole of Israel's family, and that is just Genesis. Then we have the stories of the Exodus, Naomi and Ruth, David, Elijah, and the Babylonian exile. The New Testament narratives start with a forced journey to Bethlehem, followed by fleeing to Egypt, through to Paul's final journey to Rome. Caring for others is a basic Christian principle, without the secular addition of 'as they would care for you', but it should be realised that the arrival of migrants is not a victimless activity. Those fleeing a warzone or natural disaster are obvious victims, as are those who have been tricked or forced into paying vast sums to be taken to a country that doesn't want them and does not offer whatever was promised. But there are also those working for their own ends of terrorism or to gain monetary advantage. Other victims are those who must deal with dreadful situations in this country or who are put in fear or actual harm. Some organisations have taken the migrants' side, to excess. Migrant Helpline was removed from a contract by Kent County Council for not being impartial, and they are no longer a voucher provider for Dover Foodbank because of their demand for long-term food support, against the principles of the Trussell Trust.

It is too easy to think all migrants are refugees and genuinely entitled to asylum. Here are just a few examples of the effect these arrivals can have. Port staff have had to do special checks on unaccompanied lorries in case there are people inside running out of air. This is a distressing job, waiting to find disaster. Eurotunnel drivers were scared to go to work for fear of attack or having people in front of their train and not being able to stop. As most people moved to crossing in boats, the RNLI have taken much of the brunt. The first rule of the sea is to save life, whatever the reason, but with call-outs doubling previous records, volunteers got very tired. RNLI collectors in the town started getting abuse from the public for spending so much resource on migrants who had deliberately put themselves in danger.

The lifeboat crew are having a very trying time. I never expected to hear an experienced member say he had got to the stage of dreading the pager going yet again at dawn. So many seafarers, fishermen, ferry crews, pleasure boats, are shocked and concerned at the sheer foolishness of people in small boats on dangerous waters. Many people along the coast know others who have drowned (someone I knew drowned in the harbour when I was about eleven), and it gives a continual sense of trepidation that something bad will happen.

A major concern for people in Dover is when organisations sup-porting refugees or racial justice choose Dover to stage dem-onstrations designed to get press attention, ignoring the fact it will attract right-wing groups who cause major disruption and damage to local lives and businesses.

All these encounters, and many more, highlight some of the concerns and hurt caused, albeit unintentionally, by migrants attempting illegal entry to this country and the difficulties of ministering to and caring for everybody.

 Reflection

* How is your community affected by migration near you? Are there positive and negative effects?
* How do we care for the staff and volunteers engaged in potentially traumatising work?

Looking from the White Cliffs of Dover, you can usually see the French coast just a few miles away. Kirrilee Reid worked with displaced people in Calais.

KIRRILEE'S STORY

I think it was from the age of twelve that I felt called to help people in need. My great-grandfather founded Newcastle City Mission in Australia to care for the poor, so there's always been a sense of social justice in my background. In my teenage years, the drought in Ethiopia (among other things) had a profound impact. After ordination in Australia, I later served as a priest in Scotland. I trained as a spiritual director in the Ignatian tradition, during which there was time for me to explore the 'edges' of society again. That's when my heart for refugee issues bubbled up and hasn't left. Instead of visiting Paris for our 20th wedding anniversary, my husband Ewan and I volunteered on the island of Lesvos following the Syrian refugee crisis. It was at the time when a deal between Turkey and the EU had been brokered to stop the boats coming across the Aegean to Greece. We worked with an NGO helping with very practical things, like painting walls, fixing beds or picking up rubbish, like old life jackets, from beaches. This last task was very moving as it connected with real people in crisis.

I subsequently completed training in trauma-related practices and in 2018 took a three-month sabbatical which was spent back on Lesvos, working with the Starfish Foundation, who negotiated access to Moria Refugee camp (now run by the Greek authorities). Here I taught the trauma healing classes to refugees and even camp staff. They were so desperate. The doctors were even saying, 'Please help us in any way. There are not enough professionals to support psychological issues.' I worked with predominantly young women but also traumatised young men and children. Using these gentle trauma healing and wellness exercises over time made a significant difference. This came as bit of a shock to me, as these were not miracle cures, but techniques to release some of the trapped trauma in body and mind. It was important to avoid triggers, but also to focus on releasing some of the stress and anxiety, to live a little better, each day.

Singing the Lord's song in a strange land

Someone I will never forget was a twelve-year-old girl from Iraq who was so traumatised from witnessing her father's murder that she couldn't speak or leave her mother's side. She couldn't play, wasn't eating and wouldn't even go to the toilet on her own. A couple of weeks of gentle exercises later (including singing and dancing as therapy), helping her to find a safe place to talk, I was amazed to watch her playing with a new friend outside the tent, away from her mother. These are experiences you hold on to.

I returned to the UK, and that's when the pioneering role as refugee project officer in Calais and chaplain to three Christian communities in northern France emerged. When I arrived in Calais, the notorious 'jungle' camp of refugees had been dismantled. Exiles couldn't access help and there was systematic abuse from the authorities, which we hadn't seen in Greece. This was shocking and dehumanising. It was a huge challenge for those working in the field.

I began by volunteering with a women's group and offering the same wellness exercises, when appropriate and right to do so, at other times sitting and listening. The exercises helped build connections, especially with those accessing support from the Women's Refugee Centre. Many young women and families arrived at the beginning of the summer, including a woman who had to give birth by a caesarean section at a nearby hospital. She had nowhere to go and faced returning to a tent in the 'jungle'. A Benedictine brother, who had been running a safe house in Calais, had left, needing a break from front-line ministry. Subsequently the house was closed to 'sleep' for a while. But the local community trusted me enough to reopen it. It was a response to need. It was always crisis, crisis, crisis. So we recruited more volunteers.

One of the earliest examples of why it was so important was a young Eritrean woman who'd made her way through Malta to France. She had a three-year-old son, and they were living in a flimsy tent in the 'jungle'. The little boy couldn't speak; he communicated with grunts, much like an animal. His mother wasn't coping. She was traumatised and unable to care for him. So, over the next twelve months, we supported them in the house. They were given the basics of food and shelter, but also love and patience. In a real sense, it was meeting Maslow's hierarchy (pyramid) of need. First, they were given a safe place to rest and heal, with no judgement. Then the challenge was to move to the next step. You start with healthy food, then perhaps try to teach the alphabet, then spoken language. It's not an easy road. I watched this young boy go from not being able to connect or even look at you to sitting on my knee in church, his face lighting up and him now able to give a hug, wanting to show love. It was mind-blowing to see such transformation. They are now living independently, settled in France, with the boy in school, speaking, learning and going to a local church.

I also remember three young Eritrean women. It was late December. They slept for about three weeks, only coming out of their rooms to eat. There was a transformation in them as well. They became unrecognisable from the travel-weary women who first came through the doors. They could now be seen in the kitchen, preparing food for the large household, with fun and laughter. They even provided a whole Easter feast for everyone, and made 50 loaves of bread to distribute to those in the 'jungle'. All three women are now in the UK, have had their asylum claims accepted, and I have visited them. For one young woman, her dreams of becoming a nurse might just be possible.

The sacrifice and the cost

This kind of frontline work comes at a cost, with many experiencing vicarious trauma, burnout and breakdown. You get so far into the work and the needs of others that it is hard to stop. Regular breaks are crucial, along with a balance of work and play. I've spoken to others who have had a similar experience to me. The cost of giving can be masked because you're given so much in return. You don't notice that you're becoming depleted because of the gifts that those living in exile are giving to you – hospitality, generosity and friendship. On the one hand, you don't notice this long-term pattern chipping away, because these nourishing moments sustain you. You are buoyed and feel so blessed. But when you do have an opportunity to take a break, you can be haunted by the faces of those you've left behind, who can't escape for a few hours or days. Guilt then becomes a close companion.

When we have given beyond our capacity, beyond our means, when it's physically and mentally evident, there is no other option but to stop. This is my experience of burnout. I wish I had the answers, even after all my processing. I'm not ready to go to back to Calais yet – more reflection is needed. There is still a way to go.

Kirrilee and Ewan moved to Dover, where they fostered unaccompanied asylum-seeking children (UASC).

We are currently hosting UASC who have arrived, mostly by boat, on the Kent coast. They come to us either from the port or from a local hotel. Our role is to provide short-term placements before they are hopefully given a long-term home with another local authority, somewhere in the UK. These children are told that the UK is the promised land. They have reached the 'promised land', and it's not, because the national system for permanent placements is so broken that they end up staying with us for much longer. Sadly, it is also the reality that many don't end up with a foster family at all but go straight into independent living. We must absorb their disappointment. At this moment, I'm experiencing the heartbreak of this with a young Iraqi boy. I also worry that we are building up an unrealistic expectation of what another home could look like. Hopefully, we offer a space to heal from the trauma. But we live in a limbo space with these children, and that's not a good space. Being in limbo, in this situation, is uncomfortable and often unpleasant.

We need to understand what is within our power and what is not, and to be honest. We wish we could offer a 'happily ever after' scenario, but we can't. All we can say is, 'You will be safe for as long as you need to be here.' It's about naming a reality that we cannot shy away from. First, because language is so limited, we must be blunt. And second, we are watching the brokenness of a 15-year-old boy when we can't give him the answer that he wants. It's heart-breaking.

> **We need to understand what is within our power and what is not, and to be honest.**

This space is a different space from the work in Calais, because here they think they've reached the end of the road, having arrived on our shores, but there's still more to come. Calais was just a stopping-off point. Here, in our home in Dover, we are a place to rest on the way. But the other day one of the boys came and sat with me and just cried and cried. All he could say was 'Mum, Mum'. He felt safe enough and able to cry.

The only way I could do this work long-term is if I have time set aside, alone to process, because I am an introvert. Our eldest son returned home recently and said, 'Right, what's next? It's time for you to settle down now, you need to stop trying to save the world. You're getting to that age where you need to grow up. You've done your time.'

Settle down? What could that even look like? And I said, 'I don't think I'll ever be able to settle down. That's not us. We follow a call.'

— — — — — — — — — — —

Reflection

- What role does sacrifice play in welcoming the stranger?
- How much of our lives should we give and how much hold back?
- When has radical hospitality made an impact upon your life? Either as a receiver or a giver?
- 'To give and not to count the cost.' Can one give too much? What did Jesus say about it?

Our current Anglican refugee support lead in Calais is Bradon. In the first few days in his post, he witnessed trauma and death. Here are his descriptions of just two days in Calais.

BRADON'S STORY

7 October 2023

This past Sunday, while attending the commemoration for a man hit and killed by a train in Calais, we heard of yet another death. A man had drowned in a canal in Loon-Plage near Dunkerque. Together they are the 378th and 379th people to die stranded on the Anglo-Franco border since records began to be kept by the associations in 1999. We never want to reduce people to numbers, but not to keep count would only further reduce the memory of these image-bearers of God – lives full of hope, suffering, love and shattered dreams.

It's important to recognise and remember that many more have disappeared in the channel – the missing, the presumed dead, the unreported, the unidentified. The people we hear and speak so little about are usually only the ones whose bodies have been found. Since I started this new role, four people's lives have been cut short in a period of just ten days.

At 5.40 am on 26 September, the body of a young woman, 24 years old, washed up on the beach in Sangatte, next to Calais. She was found by other migrants. She drowned in the channel before she ever had the chance to ask for asylum in the UK. She was from Eritrea. When we saw the news at Maria Skobtsova House later that morning, thoughts filled our minds of our two friends who left the day before, also to cross the channel. In a desperate appeal for help a video was sent to another association, Utopia 56, by those with the woman after her death. We were told by a coordinator at Refugee Woman's Centre, who had to watch the video to potentially identify her, that it wasn't one of our two friends. We haven't heard from them since, so we assume they are safe in the UK, at least for now.

On 14 September, a man around 20 years old was hit by a car and killed in Bierne, just outside of Dunkerque. His name was Jallal. We know this because we know his friends. His brother will come to bury him. So often the dead remain nameless in the few short news stories that appear. But let's say their names when we can. Their friends and families won't forget them, even if they never hear what happened to them. That's 15 people dead since January. More and more people are dying each year. Their blood cries out for justice. God forgive us.

Soon we will mark one year since French rescue services ignored numerous calls for help. Twenty-seven men, women and children cried out in terror, and then died, their pleas for help ignored as they drowned. No help was sent.

9 October 2023
All too soon, early yesterday morning another body was found, washed up on the beach between Berck and Merlimont, more than an hour's drive south of Calais. The mayor of Merlimont, Mary Bonvoisin, reported that the deceased was 'a minor, a young Eritrean', information not confirmed at this stage by the authorities. So young, potentially still a child. Children have died before him. Children will die after him if safe routes aren't opened with incredible speed. We don't know this young man's age or any details about his short life. The last woman from Eritrea drowned on 26 September of this year; she was born in 1999.

I'd like to encourage you to take a moment to think of the years you lived before 1999, and the opportunity this woman might have had for many more years after her death. This is not an exercise in guilt. We should be grateful for every moment of life, our lives, her life, and now this young man's life too.

≈≈≈ Reflections

- How do we show solidarity with those who die trying to find safety and a new life?
- What can you do today to help displaced people in need and danger?
- What are you grateful for in your life before 1999, or your life after?

Of course, strangers do not always have to arrive from abroad. There are many already living in our society who are often considered to be strange and on the margins. One example is Gypsy, Traveller and Roma (GTR) families, who are sometimes perceived with suspicion and not always welcome in the wider community. Martin has worked with GTR communities in Kent and in Luton. Now retired, he is the bishop's advisor for GTR communities in the diocese of Canterbury. Here's part of his story.

MARTIN'S STORY

Being disrupted

From the beginning, when I started to form relationships with English Romanies, I realised it was gradually changing me at a deep level. This was because the way they were living challenged my way of living and my priorities. The most important priority for them is their family relationships, which go incredibly deep. There is often a breathtaking openness to talk about the spiritual life and to explore it, drawing on dreams or spiritual experiences they've had. It's very much living from the heart, rather than from the head. Their centre of gravity is always the heart.

When I was vicar of Cranbrook, I found myself ministering in a highly educated community. Going out to the Romanies living in the parish was like going to a foreign country and back a few centuries in time and being with a people who had an entirely different worldview and way of understanding of how God works in the world.

When we moved on ten years later to Luton, alongside my parish ministry I started to work with the local Roma community who had migrated from Romania in recent times. I gradually began to learn their Romani language. I felt I was breaking into a deeper level of understanding of who these migrant Roma families were and, in a way, 'going a little bit native'. Over the next nine years I became very close to many of them. I was almost adopted into their families. This touched a very deep place within me. Two of my brothers had died in my childhood, which had had a devastating effect on us as a family. At the time it wasn't handled well at all. Being drawn into the daily life of these close-knit Roma families was very healing.

Family relationships are so fundamental. With the Roma, it's as if time stands still. They don't go off trying to better themselves in any way. They are masters at living in the present. It is all just about being together, always together. Never ever would you find a Roma person on their own through their own choice. Being with them was like stepping back to the other side of the Enlightenment and entering a medieval culture.

I increasingly began to feel that going about living my Christian faith in the way I was, was really a bit of an indulgence. And it was so superficial. The call of the gospel to go out to the poor, the needy and the marginalised is not a bolt-on. It's totally central to the gospel narrative and to the cry of the prophets. It was as though I hadn't really understood that, until I began to realise that it's the kind of thing Jesus would be doing if he were around now. It reformed my ministry and changed me too. It's all there in Matthew 25:31–46 – the discovery of Jesus in the face of the homeless, the prisoner, the migrant, the needy. This whole new emphasis became central to me, but it became difficult to sustain this alongside being a regular vicar. The extent to which main-stream churches involve themselves in this kind of ministry is the extent to which they will flourish. The church itself will be blessed by adopting an outward-looking ministry. It's all there in Isaiah 58!

The importance of community

I felt very blessed by engaging with GTR communities. I have to say it was extremely hard work, especially in Luton. I don't think I could have sustained what I was doing a lot longer. It was in a way impossibly demanding. The needs of the people were so much greater than any one person could respond to. I had dreamt of placing the ministry to the Roma people within a community of faith, within a group of people that would maybe even live together, share life together and support each other in this demanding ministry. I did try to set that up, but it just wasn't to be. I felt that if we could have a community of people with different skills and backgrounds working alongside the Roma people living in Luton, that would have been taking it to another level. Maybe that will come another time.

The music of God's mercy

A definition of this kind of ministry is trying to tap into the heart of the mercy of God. That God's heart is there already ahead of us, with the neediest people of the world, wherever they are. If you find the place where God is, and you go there and are alongside those people, then you get back more than you put into it. But it's the exchange of ideas, cultures and friendships that matters, which is best done in community. My problem was, I was always too much of a lone ranger in all these things. And I felt that the greatest progress would always have been made with others doing it alongside me. There was some of that, but not enough.

Now a group of us are building an online network of people who work with GTR communities all over the country. There are some encouraging signs of people beginning to relate to each other to share ideas, knowledge and projects.

— — — — — — — — — — —

Martin's vision, and his experience, like so many other working alongside people of diverse cultures is like a musical encounter where different voices are distinct and yet blend together to create beautiful relationships, where the music of the whole is greater than the sum of its parts. Such polyphony can only happen when there is genuine listening and empathetic response from all sides, so that individual biases and egos become subservient to the ebb and flow of communal sound, for the common good.

 ## Reflection

- Has your life ever been challenged by being with those who are different to you?
- Where do you find a sense of belonging?
- Where might the music of God's mercy be in your local area?

 ## A prayer

Incarnate loving Jesus, born as a refugee,
grant us your gifts of compassion and welcome
for the homeless and hungry who have fled from oppression, war and danger.
Help us to overcome fear and prejudice that we may share the abundance of your generosity with strangers seeking refuge and asylum.
Bless the work of all those who walk alongside refugees,
comfort and bless all those adversely affected by refugee arrivals on our shores,
and may the light of your love be known to all. Amen.

🌿 A spiritual exercise

Prepare yourself for prayer

Sit comfortably with both feet on the ground and hands open on your lap as if waiting to receive a gift from God. Let go of your worries or thoughts and entrust yourself and everything to God. Pray that you will be receptive to what God has to say to you in this scripture reading.

Read the passage below out loud, slowly and meditatively. Listen for words or phrases that speak to you. Sit with it for a while.

> And if a stranger sojourn with thee in your land, ye shall not vex him. But the stranger that dwelleth with you shall be unto you as one born among you, and thou shalt love him as thyself; for ye were strangers in the land of Egypt: I am the Lord your God.
> LEVITICUS 19:33–34 (KJV)

Meditate

Read these verses again. This time, let the words or phrases that stood out for you the first time become an invitation from God to speak with him. Allow the words to flow through you as you meditate upon them.

Pray

Now read the passage a third time, slowly.

Ask

- What is God saying to you in these words?
- What do you want to say to God?
- What feelings are stirred within you?
- Share your answers with God.

Contemplate

Read the text one last time, and this time let the words you have been praying with go free. Be still and at peace with God.

Ask

- What gift has God given you to take away?
- What action might God be inviting you to undertake?
- Thank God for this gift and for his invitation.

Further resources

Helen T. Boursier, *Willful Ignorance: Overcoming the limitations of (Christian) love for refugees seeking asylum* (Lexington Books, 2022).

Helen. T. Boursier, *Desperately Seeking Asylum: Testimonies of trauma, courage, and love* (Rowman and Littlefield, 2019).

Martin Burrell, *One New Humanity: Spiritual reflections on the Luton Roma* (Authorhouse, 2020).

Martin Burrell, *The Pure in Heart: An epistle from the Romanies* (Authorhouse, 2009).

Diocese of Canterbury, 'Myth-busting: refugees and asylum seekers', **churchofengland.org/sites/default/files/2023-07/myth-busting-refugees-and-asylum-seekers.pdf**

Diocese of Canterbury, 'Working with refugees', **canterburydiocese. org/mission/faith-in-action/working-with-refugees/working-with-refugees**

Tobin Hansen and María Engracia Robles Robles (eds), *Voices of the Border: Testimonios of migration, deportation, and asylum* (Georgetown University Press, 2021).

Steven Horne, *Gypsies and Jesus: A traveller theology* (Darton, Longman and Todd, 2022).

Fleur S. Houston, *You Shall Love the Stranger as Yourself: The Bible, refugees and asylum* (Routledge, 2015).

Gil Loescher, *Refugees: A very short introduction* (Oxford University Press, 2021).

Alastair Redfern, *Slavery and Salvation* (ISPCK, 2020).

Susanna Snyder, *Asylum-seeking, Migration and Church* (Ashgate, 2012).

The Clewer Initiative, 'A community of compassion', 27 June 2023, **theclewerinitiative.org/blog/a-community-of-compassion**

8

INNER HARMONY, HEALTH AND HEALING: VISITING THE SICK

███████████████████████

'I was sick and you took care of me.'
MATTHEW 25:36

As soon as they left the synagogue, they entered the house of Simon and Andrew, with James and John. Now Simon's mother-in-law was in bed with a fever, and they told him about her at once. He came and took her by the hand and lifted her up. Then the fever left her, and she began to serve them.

That evening, at sunset, they brought to him all who were sick or possessed by demons. And the whole city was gathered around the door. And he cured many who were sick with various diseases and cast out many demons, and he would not permit the demons to speak, because they knew him.
MARK 1:29–34

Care of the sick must rank above and before all else, so that they may truly be served as Christ, for he said: I was sick and you visited me (Matthew 25:36), and, What you did for one of these least brothers you did for me (Matthew 25:40). Let the sick on their part bear in mind that they are served out of honour for God, and let them not by their excessive demands distress their brothers who serve them. Still, sick brothers must be patiently borne with, because serving them leads to a greater reward. Consequently, the abbot should be extremely careful that they suffer no neglect. Let a separate room be designated for the sick, and let them be served by an attendant who is God-fearing, attentive and concerned. The sick may take baths whenever it is advisable, but the healthy, and especially the young, should receive permission less readily. Moreover, to regain their strength, the sick who are very weak may eat meat, but when their health improves, they should all abstain from meat as usual. The abbot must take the greatest care that cellarers and those who serve the sick do not neglect them, for the shortcomings of disciples are his responsibility.

The Rule of St Benedict, chapter 36

We cannot forget the tender love and perseverance of many families in caring for their chronically sick or severely disabled children, parents and relatives. The care given within families is an extraordinary witness of love for the human person; it needs to be acknowledged and supported by suitable policies.

Pope Francis[56]

Music has often been used a source of healing; from comforting the unquiet heart, or unlocking memories and melodies from a mind troubled with dementia, it has long been known to help soothe pain and release creativity. Music touches every aspect of our humanity, mind and soul. From the neurological to the physiological, from the physical to the emotional, from the experiential to the spiritual, music can work holistically as a therapeutic tool. Just as communal making of music brings people together, so the internalisation and embodiment of music as an individual can bring inner harmony, healing and peace. The musical metaphor of harmony reminds us of ancient ideas, such as the music of the spheres – that Pythagorean notion that the movement of the planets, in accordance with the divine plan, created music. We use the metaphor of harmony to describe God himself in the unity of the Trinity.

Harmony and healing can be helpful ways of thinking about this work of mercy, visiting the sick, especially if we see health as multifaceted, involving all aspects of our humanity, not just our physical health. That is why the simple act of visiting can be so beneficial in the healing process and in helping others find a way to inner harmony. No one knows this more than those on the front line of hospital care, and especially hospital chaplains. We're going to hear from one such chaplain who found that this ministry was the most rewarding and important in his entire life of pastoral care. As we have seen earlier in this book, this ministry involves the kind of interrupting, improvising and composing that we find in music and musical performance. These three elements combine to help provide a holistic understanding of harmony and healing within the context of hospital care. It is a vocational and creative process, which is deeply fulfilling, as Dominic explains.

> **The simple act of visiting can be so beneficial in the healing process and in helping others find a way to inner harmony.**

DOMINIC'S STORY

For me, those 14 years were the most formative of my ministry of 36 years so far and probably the most important. That's not to set aside any of the other things I have done or what I'm doing now. Someone asked me recently what had been the most important part of my ministry. And I said, without even thinking, my time as a hospital chaplain and caring for people in that environment. And when asked, 'Why was that?' my answer had to be, because I felt then that I was doing what I was really ordained to do.

Since the inception of the NHS in 1948, chaplains like myself have been part of its story. There was a time when a chaplain might be summoned to take tea with Matron, followed perhaps by a perambulation around the ward, to console, to support, to inspire patients who might require a long period in hospital for recuperation, recovery or rest. But those days are long gone. Matron no longer hosts afternoon tea. And even if there were such a thing, the chaplain would be unlikely to be able to attend – such is the pace of hospital life now. The NHS has changed. Chaplaincy has changed – and the resources, of course, are far less bountiful now than anyone might imagine.

Interruptions

The challenge of my own world as a hospital chaplain, for some 14-plus years, was as diverse as any occupation could be, as I rushed to respond to the constant demands of the 'bleep' of my pager, the number of which the switchboard, the matrons and the director of nursing all knew. If ever you wanted the chaplain, you would bleep – and it went and it went and it went as I rushed from one place to another. And its call could take me from the bedside of the young 23-year-old brought lifeless into casualty, to the equally young mother with breast cancer whose prognosis was poor, to the bedside of the loving father of three young children whose sudden brain haemorrhage had placed him on life support, or to the man with a once incredible memory, now diminished by dementia and unable to recognise his devoted wife of 48 years. These were just a handful of the literally hundreds if not thousands of encounters I experienced in my years as a hospital chaplain. Professional, skilled and able chaplains continue to respond 24/7 today. And as a parish priest, I now surmise how easy is the life of the parochial clergy when compared with those who for 12, sometimes 18, hours a day (and often with little sleep if you're on call), nevertheless enable the ministry of the church to be worked out in our hospitals, hospices and care facilities up and down the land.

Holistic ministry

Chaplains hold such a privileged role, it seems to me, and are able to do the work they do precisely because the founders of the modern NHS had the wisdom and common sense to see that health, as defined by the World Health Organization, is a 'state of complete physical, mental, spiritual and social well-being and not merely the absence of disease or infirmity'[57] – and I think that's a very important point. Clinicians deal with disease and infirmity. Chaplains, together with mental health and other allied health professionals, pick up much of the rest. And not only for patients, but also for their relatives and increasingly for hospital staff members too.

For in hospital, and away from the comforts of home and the society of family and friends, the patient journey is not always an easy one, especially for those confronting serious or life-threatening illness or injury. In hospital, and away from their familiar routines, people often face ultimate questions about life and death. They search for meaning in the experience of suffering, loss, loneliness, anxiety, impairment. And they are often forced to address, perhaps in many cases for the first time, the realities of the human condition. All these things play a crucial part in the journey towards wellness. Chaplains are both trained and skilled in responding to these needs.

Often chaplains meet people at a point where what we might call their secure mini-narrative has come unstuck through illness. And constantly, what we try to do is to help people to find their own narrative again, to be able to feel as though they are the tellers of their own story – and not simply the focus of the narrative of the clinicians treating them.

Chaplains, of course, also help to anchor the mini-narrative of hospital staff too, whose lives are just as fragmented as those of the patients they serve. Indeed, if I tell you that during my time as a hospital chaplain, we encountered two or three suicides among members of staff, you will not be surprised to hear that healthcare practitioners themselves are not immune from the issues faced by the rest of society.

Chaplains, too, are human beings, and they are also sometimes adrift with perhaps no overarching story to secure them. And even though they might feel secure in their own sense of vocation and calling to ministry within the health service, they are aware that their narrative is not always convincing, or even comprehensible, to many of the people among whom they work. I think that's probably true for those who work in any secular type of ministry.

Improvisation

When I joined the NHS, I'd never been a hospital chaplain before. There were some 2,000 staff in the hospital in which I worked, and about 500 inpatients at any one time. Many of the people I encountered came from non-religious, non-faith backgrounds. Therefore, the expectations people have of you as the chaplain, and of your role within the institution, are perhaps limited. So you must determine, early on, what your role is going to be and how you're going to relate within that context. The church helps you to some degree, together with your training or background. But it was interesting in the first two or three weeks that I was there that the pager hardly ever bleeped.

I think it may be that chaplains spend perhaps too much time trying to justify their existence in what is ostensibly a secular environment. They try to justify not only their existence, but also perhaps their pay cheque! Like other healthcare professionals, they must gather data, design questionnaires, submit to 'performance management', manage people themselves, with budgets and volunteers, talk about customer satisfaction and management practices in a way that often sits oddly with their identity as priests or ministers. This is not of course what most chaplains went into it for, any more than it is what most doctors and nurses went into it for. And consequently, roles are misunderstood or not understood at all. There may be less and less quality time available, not least for qualitative, dignified and decent patient care. And those known to me, who have been in hospital as patients recently, tell me that this is *their* experience of their own hospital stay, by and large. We must ask, how long such future care, free at the point of access for all, will remain sustainable?

What then, in practical terms, do hospital chaplains do? Several things characterised much of my daily routine: trauma care; critical care; end-of-life care; liaising (often on behalf of families and with family members) with organ donation and transplantation teams; bereavement support; weddings.

People actually get married in hospital. This is often, sadly, only when a patient is unlikely to survive. I once took a wedding in hospital where the couple had lived together for some 40 years, but they had never actually got married. Now the doctors had determined that the patient had a life expectancy of only about three weeks. If they didn't get married quickly, their partner was set to lose the home and everything they had built up together over many years. Hospitals, of course, unlike churches, aren't licenced places. So, if you face that sort of situation, you've got to move quickly – contact the local Registry Office (or Lambeth Palace) to try to get a special marriage licence (perhaps for the palliative care room where the wedding is to take place), and to do that quickly is a challenge. Time is of the essence. So that's one of the things which several times I was involved in and had to arrange.

Then, there is neonatal and maternity support. Fortunately, not many children are lost in childbirth these days, but it does happen. And it happened especially in that area of London where I worked, where there's a lot of poverty – sometimes with people living under the radar in deprived circumstances, perhaps without an official identity and, consequently, no automatic right to NHS treatment. Then they suddenly fall sick, and someone brings them to the hospital. So there's all that to deal with – as well as funerals, if such a patient (without ID) doesn't survive. If someone dies in hospital, whether on a ward or even just in the parking lot, and they do not have relatives or the means to arrange their own funeral, it is the responsibility of the NHS Trust to arrange and pay for a decent funeral service and cremation or burial, and for the hospital chaplain to take the service.

Composition

Then there are chapel services, of course, and staff support, induction training for new team members too. I was also involved in training for nurses – and one of the things I did was to set up a course called 'Breaking bad news'. Newly qualified personnel are not always the best people to tell a patient they have a life-threatening or even terminal condition, and the way in which that's done is understandably very important. So, I set up a whole series of role-play afternoons when nurses, some of the new doctors and other healthcare professionals would take part in role play, as we teased out some of the issues involved in 'What is it like to hear bad news?'

Then there are the almost daily questions: 'Why has God let this happen to me?' or 'Why is the world against me?' These are questions which chaplains meet every day, and we must always be very careful not to give easy or glib answers. For often, of course, there just are no answers. I'm sorry if that sounds like a cop-out, but it's true! Christian faith for me leaves almost as many questions as it provides answers.

The chaplain is there first and foremost to try to help people find meaning, value and purpose within the context of the patient's current narrative, and to find hope and strength within it. That may not always be possible. But it is *never* the role of a chaplain, or of anyone within the chaplaincy team, to evangelise. In fact, I almost find the suggestion offensive!

Yet over time, I've come to realise that sector chaplains need to be better theologians and stronger in their faith than those who work within more recognised church structures, such as parochial ministry. For existing church structures usually support and understand theology and faith in a way in which secular institutions overall don't.

Most people would probably say that they would like to end their days in the comfort of their own bed, in their own home and surrounded by those things which have given their lives meaning. Sadly, a recent report notes that increasingly large numbers of people who die every year in this country do so in either a hospital or a care home. Lack of funding for community-based end-of-life care must be a large reason for that, together with the increasing breakdown of traditional family-based support structures. Those are the two main things which I think stop people being able to have their final weeks of life in the place where they would most want to be.

Vocation

I would without doubt describe hospital chaplaincy as 'vocation'. Priests and ministers working in our hospitals have a clear sense of vocation, albeit different to that owned by the parochial clergy, not least through living and working alongside serious illness, trauma and death. In my own hospital tenure, it was not unusual for me to attend six or seven deaths in a single day and among people of all ages and situations. It is a ministry with a distinctive charism, whereby one is required to travel with many people, of all faiths and none, along what is often a difficult road. Yet life for me as a hospital chaplain has been one of the greatest privileges of my life and the thing I hope will ultimately define my ministry.

Finally, the NHS (which promised at its inception to make available holistic professional medical and nursing care for every single inhabitant of these islands, from 'the cradle to the grave') is having to adapt more than ever before to a changing world and to a dramatically changed political, economic and financial climate. The NHS is no longer affordable. That is what we're being told. And we are going to have to look to provide more for ourselves as we get older. The founders of the NHS in 1948 could not have pictured for a minute the advances, the developments and the changes that we have seen. But if the NHS is to survive, and if chaplaincy and the provision of professional holistic pastoral and spiritual care is to survive as part of healthcare provision, then it will need constantly to be reminded of two timeless truths.

First, that as human beings, each of us is a wonderful combination of the physical, the mental, the social and the spiritual. And second, that to heal the sick – to make people well again – is indeed a vocation, a true collaboration with the creator God, from whom ultimately, all true health and wholeness comes.

> **To heal the sick – to make people well again – is indeed a vocation, a true collaboration with the creator God.**

 Reflections

- Have you ever spent a long time in hospital, either for your own health or that of a friend or relative? What did you learn?
- There are many kinds of sickness and many kinds of health. What do you ask God to heal in you today?

Another holistic ministry beneficial to heart, mind and soul, is that of Anna Chaplaincy, helping people to find inner healing, wholeness and harmony in later life. The ministry's name is taken from the prophet Anna in Luke's gospel:

There was also a prophet, Anna the daughter of Phanuel, of the tribe of Asher. She was of a great age, having lived with her husband seven years after her marriage, then as a widow to the age of eighty-four. She never left the temple but worshipped there with fasting and prayer night and day. At that moment she came and began to praise God and to speak about the child to all who were looking for the redemption of Jerusalem.
LUKE 2:36–38

Julia is Anna Chaplaincy lead for Rochester and Canterbury dioceses and is also Anna Chaplaincy training and development lead for BRF Ministries.

JULIA'S STORY

Spiritual care

Anna Chaplaincy is spiritual care for older people. It is community based and is a ministry of the local church to older people in their locality. For people who have a faith and have been church members, it's about sustaining and supporting them in that faith and helping them stay connected to the local church family. For those who don't have a connection, we're very much person-centred in how we come alongside them. We start from where they are in their lives and we look at the spiritual questions of meaning, purpose, belonging and hope, which in later life can seem urgent. We define spiritual care more broadly than religious care. We're all spiritual beings, so we come alongside people to listen to their stories and help them work through those bigger issues in their lives.

Story-tellers and music-makers

Sometimes this involves people in the task of looking back over their life, making sense of it, looking at the different parts of their story, and trying to figure out meaning and purpose. How did my life match up to what I thought it would be? What areas of life do I need to work through, and do I need to reconcile myself to people or ask them to forgive me? Anna Chaplaincy is about coming alongside people for that part of their journey, helping them to express some of their feelings about their lives, maybe some of their deepest fears about death and dying and what happens after they're gone, and the legacy they've left behind. These are things that older people want to talk about, but don't always have a partner with whom they feel comfortable discussing those things. People often feel reluctant to talk to their family members, so a chaplain is there to be the person that helps them articulate and work through their fears.

A valued ministry

This ministry is very much valued because the broad intention of it is love and kindness, which is recognised by the older person who is often isolated. To have someone who is just there to listen and be alongside is like gold dust in our society.

Human value and dignity

A strong message for me is that older people have a huge amount still to give spiritually, relationally and in many other ways. Anna was the one who went and told people about her encounter with Jesus. She was tireless in her vocation. So we're trying to challenge the idea that when you're retired you're no longer productive. We must be concerned about the way in which local and national government provide for older people.

It's difficult not to be pessimistic at the moment, because we're facing such difficult and uncertain times as a nation. We celebrate ageing, but there are implications for our welfare and healthcare resources, many of which are used by older people. The advances of modern science and medicine enable people to live longer, but there are vast discrepancies in care provision around the country. Pensioner poverty is much higher in some parts of the country than others. But I also think there's hope that we can still provide a welfare safety net that allows people to flourish in their later years. There's another hope – that more churches will appoint specialist, older people's ministers to look out for those who most need help and support. There are an increasing number of older people who don't have close friends or family to care for them. It's dangerous to think that it's for the welfare state to look after our elderly mums and dads. It was never intended that the state do everything. We rely very heavily on informal care, communities, families and neighbourhoods. If we hadn't been providing unpaid care over the history of the welfare state, it would have collapsed long ago.

— — — — — — — — — — —

 ## Reflections

- What does spirituality mean to you?
- Looking back on your life, where do you find purpose and meaning?
- With whom do you need reconciliation?
- Do you know anyone who is isolated or lonely in older life? How can you come alongside them?

 ## A prayer

Lord Jesus, you came to bring sight to the blind and healing to the nations. Be with all those who suffer in body, mind or spirit this day. We pray for our loved ones in distress or pain. We thank you for the work of doctors, nurses and all medical staff in the work of healing. May we ever

be mindful of those who are ill and live out your gospel in offering time, patience and care, that those who are disquieted in heart and mind may find hope, healing and inner harmony. Amen.

 ## A spiritual exercise

Prepare yourself for prayer
Sit comfortably with both feet on the ground and hands open on your lap as if waiting to receive a gift from God. Let go of your worries or thoughts and entrust yourself and everything to God. Pray that you will be receptive to what God has to say to you in this scripture reading.

Read the passage below out loud, slowly and meditatively. Listen for words or phrases that speak to you. Sit with it for a while.

Happy are those who consider the poor;
  the Lord delivers them in the day of trouble.
The Lord protects them and keeps them alive;
  they are called happy in the land.
  You do not give them up to the will of their enemies.
The Lord sustains them on their sickbed;
  in their illness you heal all their infirmities.

As for me, I said, 'O Lord, be gracious to me;
  heal me, for I have sinned against you.'
My enemies wonder in malice
  when I will die and my name perish.
And when they come to see me, they utter empty words
  while their hearts gather mischief;
  when they go out, they tell it abroad.
All who hate me whisper together about me;
  they imagine the worst for me.

They think that a deadly thing has fastened on me,
  that I will not rise again from where I lie.

Even my close friend in whom I trusted,
  who ate of my bread, has lifted the heel against me.
But you, O Lord, be gracious to me,
  and raise me up, that I may repay them.

By this I know that you are pleased with me:
  because my enemy has not triumphed over me.
But you have upheld me because of my integrity
  and set me in your presence forever.

Blessed be the Lord, the God of Israel,
  from everlasting to everlasting.
  Amen and Amen.
PSALM 41

Meditate
Read these verses again. This time, let the words or phrases that stood out for you the first time become an invitation from God to speak with him. Allow the words to flow through you as you meditate upon them.

Pray
Now read the passage a third time, slowly.

Ask
- What is God saying to you in these words?
- What do you want to say to God?
- What feelings are stirred within you?
- Share your answers with God.

Contemplate
- Read the text one last time, and this time let the words you have been praying with go free. Be still and at peace with God.

Ask
- What gift has God given you to take away?

- What action might God be inviting you do?
- Thank God for this gift and for his invitation.

Further resources

Kelly Arora, *Spirituality and Meaning Making in Chronic Illness: How spiritual caregivers can help people navigate long-term health conditions* (Jessica Kingsley, 2020).

Barbara Brown Taylor, *God in Pain: Teaching sermons on suffering* (Canterbury Press, 2013).

Christopher Chapman, *Seeing in the Dark: Pastoral perspectives on suffering from the Christian spiritual tradition* (Canterbury Press, 2018).

Bernadette Meaden, *Illness, Disability and Caring: How the Bible can help us understand* (Darton, Longman and Todd, 2020).

Lisa Pence, *Illness Observed Through Reluctant Eyes: Encouragement, ideas and anecdotes for individuals facing a serious illness as a patient or caregiver* (Morgan James, 2019).

Jennifer Tann, *Soul Pain: Priests reflect on personal experiences of serious and terminal illness* (Canterbury Press, 2013).

Alan Thomas, *Tackling Mental Illness Together: A biblical and practical approach* (IVP, 2017).

9

THE LOST AND BROKEN CHORDS: VISITING THE IMPRISONED

'I was in prison and you visited me.'
MATTHEW 25:36

They seized Paul and Silas and dragged them into the marketplace before the authorities. When they had brought them before the magistrates, they said, 'These men, these Jews, are disturbing our city and are advocating customs that are not lawful for us, being Romans, to adopt or observe.' The crowd joined in attacking them, and the magistrates had them stripped of their clothing and ordered them to be beaten with rods. After they had given them a severe flogging, they threw them into prison and ordered the jailer to keep them securely. Following these instructions, he put them in the innermost cell and fastened their feet in the stocks.

About midnight Paul and Silas were praying and singing hymns to God, and the prisoners were listening to them. Suddenly there was an earthquake so violent that the foundations of the prison were shaken, and immediately all the doors were opened and everyone's chains were unfastened. When the jailer woke up and saw the prison doors wide open, he drew his sword and was about to kill himself, since he supposed that the prisoners had escaped. But Paul shouted in a loud voice, 'Do not harm yourself, for we are all here.' The jailer called for lights, and rushing in, he fell down trembling before Paul and Silas. Then he brought them outside and said, 'Sirs, what must I do to be saved?' They answered, 'Believe in the Lord Jesus, and you will be saved, you and your household.' They spoke the word of the Lord to him and to all who were in his house. At the same hour of the night he took them and washed their wounds; then he and his entire family were baptised without delay. He brought them up into the house and set food before them, and he and his entire household rejoiced that he had become a believer in God.

ACTS 16:19–34

Remember those who are in prison, as though you were in prison with them, those who are being tortured, as though you yourselves were being tortured.

HEBREWS 13:3

Being broken is what makes us human – Our brokenness is the source of our common humanity, the basis for our shared search for comfort, meaning, and healing. Our shared vulnerability and imperfection nurtures and sustains our capacity for compassion.

Bryan Stevenson[58]

There is a song by Arthur Sullivan from the 19th century about a lost chord. It is a setting of a poem by the philanthropist Adelaide Anne Procter, who was Queen Victoria's favourite poet. Proctor's poetry is deeply influenced by her beliefs and her works of mercy with the homeless, the poor and prostitutes of London. Sullivan set the 'The Lost Chord' to music while he sat by the bedside of his dying brother, Fred. Here are the words:

Seated one day at the organ,
I was weary and ill at ease,
And my fingers wandered idly
Over the noisy keys.

I know not what I was playing
Or what I was dreaming then;
But I struck one chord of music
Like the sound of a great Amen.

It flooded the crimson twilight
Like the close of an angel's psalm,
And it lay on my fevered spirit
With a touch of infinite calm.

It quieted pain and sorrow
Like love overcoming strife;
It seemed the harmonious echo
From our discordant life.

It linked all perplexèd meanings
Into one perfect peace,
And trembled away into silence
As if it were loth to cease.

I have sought, but I seek it vainly,
That one lost chord divine,
Which came from the soul of the organ
And entered into mine.

It may be that death's bright angel
Will speak in that chord again;
It may be that only in Heav'n
I shall hear that grand Amen.

In this song a chord entered the soul of the musician which had the ability to calm strife and create inner harmony. But somehow the chord is lost and never found again. These words remind me of precious humans, born with the God-given gift of love, who sometimes, because of life's hardships, can become lost and broken. In the desperation of their pain, they often choose badly for themselves and become outcasts from society, whether through family breakdown, addiction, gang warfare or whatever route led to crime, ending up in jail. While society locks them away, God still sees that child preciously made and loved.

Like the lost chord that quieted pain and sorrow, like overcoming strife, hearing that perfect harmony of the divine can be almost impossible for some people. In this work of mercy we consider how, whether Christian or not, we might help the prisoner in some small way to hear the music of heaven and help those who have been broken to find healing and hope for themselves again. For we are all called to live connected to the lives and circumstances of others. Contrary to ideas of independence and individualism promoted by modern popular culture, we live interdependently in a society where the 'common good' requires our sympathy, understanding and goodwill, indeed mercy.

In prison the amount of individual control one has is extremely limited. As a visitor, our time in prison is, by definition, brief and we can look forward to returning to 'normal' life outside. But the writer to the Hebrews warns us away from simply being observers of someone else's misfortune. We are to have such empathy with those in prison as if we were in prison ourselves, feel the torture as they have been tortured.

But once again we must avoid the idea that the act of mercy is a gift from the bystander to the one suffering. As the testimony of Nick Ash below suggests, we are surprised by God time and time again that he is already at work, not where we might expect him to be – in the church, the affluent, polite society – but with those seen as the least in our society. In prison, where is Christ? He *is* the prisoner: 'I was in prison and you visited me… As you did it to one of the least of these brothers and sisters of mine, you did it to me' (Matthew 25:36, 40). And as his manifesto in chapter four of Luke's gospel proclaims, his ministry is biased towards the least privileged in our world – the materially, psychologically, emotionally and spiritually poor. He brings freedom from oppression and release to the captive.

In the passage from Acts 16 above, we read that Paul and Silas were indeed tortured and imprisoned. But their release does not come from any external benefaction. We find God at work in them in the middle of the jail, as they captivate the other captives with their songs of praise. God's power releases them and ironically it is they who minister and console their captor, the jailor, who begs for advice as he sees no way of carrying on living. For the jailor, he will either die from the natural disaster of the earthquake or die by his own sword from the shame of their escape and his dereliction of duty. Attempted suicide and suicidal thoughts are sadly common in prisons because people cannot see hope for the future. But there is always hope: the melody of God's mercy can do more than we can possibly imagine. When visiting the prisoner, we may not be able to bring release, but God is present especially in the darkest situations. We, like every prisoner and every prison guard, can experience this hope through God's grace working in all of us.

We are not different to the prisoner, as Nick Ash reveals from his experience: 'There but for the grace of God go any of us.' Revd Ian Cohen knows this: 'Acts of mercy, and especially that act of visiting those in prison, cannot be carried out by bystanders. They are carried out by those who know their own need, their own… despair, and total human misery.'[59]

We may not all visit those who live life behind bars, but we probably all know people who live within prisons of their own making or of their own interior reality. Perhaps we need to attend and listen to our own human nakedness. What is our own imprisonment, what is our torture? Engaging in acts of mercy is not about receiving gratitude or reward. It is about mutuality,

Engaging in acts of mercy is about mutuality, relationship, empathy and joining in with where God is already at work.

relationship, empathy and joining in with where God is already at work. As the writer to the Hebrews expressed, this involves mutual love between us and God, and neighbour with neighbour. Nick is a prison chaplain and here is his story, and also his song.

NICK'S STORY

In 2010 I was ordained a priest in the Church of England. My days as a teacher were drawing to a close after 24 years in the classroom. As I pondered where God might be leading me to next, I decided it might be an interesting experience to see what working in prisons as a chaplain would be like. It was this decision that led me to do a work placement at a prison in the south-east of England, a decision that changed the whole course of my life.

The experience of being inside a prison and taking part in the work of the chaplaincy department was powerful. There was a really strong sense of God's peace and unconditional love pervading the work of the chaplaincy department. I felt this especially during the Communion services on a Sunday and at the Bible studies I attended at the mid-week meetings.

It struck me how some of the men, despite their crimes, were really wanting to know more about God. In my naivety within this new context of ministry, this surprised me. Some of the men expressed a real closeness to Jesus and a love of him already.

The juxtaposition of two ends of a spectrum, as I saw it back then – the world of criminality and that of being a Christian – fascinated me. I thought they would be in need of the knowledge of God's salvation, but many already expressed a living and vibrant faith.

In my naive arrogance, I thought that being a priest in that environment would be the channel through which God would bring salvation to these lost souls. What I quickly realised was that God was already there inside the walls of the prison working out his purposes.

There were people who had already discovered the grace and unconditional love of God and who spoke to their fellow prisoners about it. It was a very exciting place to be. I distinctly remember kneeling at the altar one Sunday morning, receiving the bread and wine from the chaplain alongside convicted criminals on my right and my left, feeling a sense that we were all here together, kneeling as equals before the grace of God; all of us in need of God's love and forgiveness. 'For all have sinned and fall short of the glory of God', as we are reminded in Paul's letter to the Romans (3:23, NIV).

It was at this time that I began to form the conviction that God might be calling me into prison ministry. I felt I wanted to be in a place where God was at work with the marginalised and outcasts of society. Ten years into this work, mission and ministry has become for me not so much the idea of taking Jesus to the lost, but finding out where God is already at work and then joining in. It wasn't until 2013, though, when my first opportunity came to apply for a position as a chaplain in a jail for young offenders.

Working among teenagers whose lives were as far removed from mine as the sun is from the moon was quite a challenge. How could I ever relate to gangland teenagers from London, convicted of murder, attempted murder, rape, burglary, grievous bodily harm and drug trafficking? I had very little experience. I grew up in a sheltered, white, middle-class environment in a south-east London borough and then later taught in a school for 24 years whose main ethnic group was white middle- or working-class families.

But when God calls, he also equips, and I found myself filled with a courage that was not my own that enabled me to approach these young people and begin building relationships with them. A conversation would often start with that overused phrase 'How are you?' or 'Which part of the country are you from?'

Once, I asked one young lad where he lived and he said he was from a borough of London close to where I used to live. I tried to find common ground with him and said that I used to live in the next-door borough. He immediately turned and said to me, 'That place is full of pagans!' In gangland culture 'pagans' are the enemy, so I had to quickly reassure him that it was okay and that I was not a gang leader. I hardly looked like one in my dog collar and grey clerical shirt!

I stayed there for six years, spending many hours playing card games and table tennis with the young people, building a rapport with them and learning to enjoy their company. I became very good at pool and would challenge the boys and beat them time and again. Over the years their trust in me began to grow and what seemed to make the difference then, and still does in the adult jail where I work today, is the fact that I had the time to just be with these young people. I had the time to ask that question, 'How are you?', and look them in the eye and give them the time to respond. I had time to probe a little deeper and listen to their response, and then go with the flow of the conversation. I learned how to listen to the voice of God within the conversations, asking him for wisdom as I listened to what answers might be appropriate or needed at that moment.

One 16-year-old said to me once that when she was outside living her criminal lifestyle, involved in drugs, partying and clubbing, her life was just so busy, she had no time to think of anything other than herself. Now here she was faced with a man in a dog collar, and she took the opportunity to ask about faith in God. She said to me that she would never have asked such questions outside, but because I was there she took the opportunity to think a little deeper about life and its meaning.

Each Sunday I led a Christian act of worship service, guitar in hand, with disaffected teenagers worshipping a God they had only come across possibly at their primary school or maybe through some home tuition. It was a highlight in my week. I had to hold the same service multiple times, because you couldn't mix the units where the young people lived together, for fear they might fight each other. It was a place where we could speak of the God who cares for their individual needs and loves them in a way that they had never been loved before. We talked about the God in Jesus who is prepared to forgive them.

Sometimes I found myself saying to youngsters who wondered why they were in prison or were missing home or missing their freedom that maybe God had been involved in their life and they just hadn't realised it. That maybe it was God who had taken them out of the situation they were in, because if they'd stayed where they were they might well have been dead by now, and that maybe God had a better plan for their life, and that maybe the conversation that we were having then was actually all part of their story that would lead them to a more positive way of life and living.

Could this conversation, or the fact they were in prison, be an answer to their heartfelt cry for help, their cry of 'Where are you, God?' I had many conversations with these young people about forgiveness and whether they could be forgiven by God for the crimes they had committed. It was such a privilege to bring this message of hope to their young lives and watch them grapple with these deep theological truths we can share as Christian ministers of the gospel.

These conversations have continued into the adult jail where I currently work. Some of the conversations are about whether they can forgive themselves for what they have done. I remember teaching a Bible study about the golden rule to love your neighbour as you love yourself. One of the prisoners said to me,

'But I don't love myself, so how can I love my neighbour?' There was a genuine desire in him to find peace within his heart again.

So many of them lack this peace, having come from such troubled backgrounds. I come across prisoners, time and again, who have genuine remorse for what they have done with a guilt that gnaws away at their consciences. There is a genuine desire to make amends and rectify the wrongs they've committed so they can feel good again about themselves. The guilt some of them feel clings to them like mud, and they don't know how to make themselves feel better, which is why, I guess, some turn to religion in jail or they start thinking again about a faith that they had earlier on in their life.

At the jail for juveniles, I had one young man, in jail for murder, who came regularly to both Bible studies and the worship. He became very passionate about God and even began to draw others into the chaplaincy services. One Easter I had prepared an 'Experience Easter' event where you have prayer stations and walk round from place to place, looking at pictures of the Easter story and reading the description underneath of what that picture is meant to be about. He was going around each one and he stopped at a picture depicting the cross with red petals that I had put in front of it to depict the blood of Christ. He sat there for ages and ages. I looked over to him and noticed that he was weeping.

Here was a young man who had come to a place of remorse through his own journey of faith while with us, and he brought his guilt before God. At that moment he found God's wonderful grace poured out on him as he shed tears over his actions. But more importantly, shedding tears over the fact that he knew God loved him in that moment. In Jesus, his sin had been forgiven. That young man has subsequently written to me and is now working for an organisation that works with young people in the community to steer them away from a criminal lifestyle.

There was another young man who came to chapel regularly. He had many problems, but one day during his time with us, he asked if he could be baptised. So we organised some time together where we shared what the Christian faith means and what it means to be a follower of Jesus. Eventually we organised the baptism service. I went to the local garden centre and bought a huge plant pot which would become our font; I couldn't get a pool big enough to dunk him right under. We invited his family members and his friends to the service, and we had the most joyous service where he committed his life to following Jesus.

When he eventually left the prison, he went to another jail. I eventually caught up with him when I discovered that he had gone to another prison in the Midlands. I happened to be on a course nearby, and so I went along to give him a surprise visit. I was taken to his cell door, and I saw him sitting on his cell bed, smoking with his cellmate. The room was tiny with a bed and a toilet and a little shelf on the wall. He looked up and clocked who I was, then ran with his arms outstretched and gave me a huge hug. He said, 'Nick, what are you doing here?' I said, 'I've come to see how you are.' He invited me into his cell and, as we sat on his bed, I looked at the wall of his cell. All the photographs that were taken at his baptism were decorating his cell wall. He said, 'Nick, look, I've got the Bible here and I still read it. I've done the Alpha course and I still go to the chapel. I've even been inviting others to do the same.' We just don't realise the impact of the seeds that we sow.

I constantly find it amazing that all I have done in my work is just spend time with people as the prison visitor, listening to their angst, listening to their anger, listening to their depression and their strong desire to be forgiven by God. Listening and enjoying people's company creates opportunities for wonderful moments of space, sacred space even, where God begins to transform lives.

What I have found working in prisons as a Christian is that God often uses us as conduits of grace for somebody who needs it at that moment when you meet them in a corridor or on a landing, when someone is feeling particularly unloved or marginalised, or when someone needs reassurance that they are lovable and all is not lost. Most of all, the grace given is through sharing the fact that there is always hope. Hope is our watchword in prison ministry. There is always hope. God is a God of hope, of forgiveness and second chances, and prisoners need to be able to hear that. So many prisoners want to know that they have a future.

We have to deal with prisoners who try to hang themselves. They might even try to poison themselves. Sometimes they will do anything to end their life, because they can't cope with the awfulness of their situation. We as chaplains and other prison staff bring around them a support team at that moment, and we say, 'It's going to be okay. There is a future beyond this crisis. Lean on us. And we'll be here for you and help you through.'

What I often see in each prisoner I talk to is still that little boy inside who wasn't loved as a youngster as he ought to have been loved. Things went badly wrong in his younger years, and the way he should have been taught to live was not taught to him and he ended up living the life that got him into jail. One prisoner told me a year or so ago that he got into crime because one Christmas his dad pushed him through a window and said to him, 'Get your own presents!' What chance did that boy have for a life of love, warmth, kindness, gentleness and care?

Another story I heard was of a young man, now in his mid-20s, aged twelve, who got caught up with county lines drugs trafficking. The gang leaders encouraged him to join them and that they'd help him find some boys of his own age to play with. What happened was he got taken to another town where he stayed guarding a drug den. For two years his parents had no idea where he was. There he was, caught up in the world of drugs, and the rest is history!

Some of these young men and adults had very little chance to start out well. Listening to their stories sometimes makes your toes curl, but listening to them has really helped me appreciate my life and my upbringing. To those who have been given much, much is expected. God has blessed me with faith in Jesus and a loving family. I feel called to share that love and faith with those who have not had the chance to experience it for themselves. So, when I meet prisoners, I don't ask, 'Why are you in jail?' I don't judge them for being there. There but for the grace of God go any of us. I see them for who they are. I see human beings who need love. Human beings who need to know something of the unconditional nature of God's love which has the power to transform their lives. I see people who weren't loved as children, but need to know how much the heavenly Father loves them and wants the very best for them.

Society wants to lock them away and throw away the key. As a Christian, though, in that environment, I can say that God is present in them. He's in the midst of their troubles and he does have a grander plan for their lives, much more than the world would allow for.

I don't see prison ministry as something that can be measured by what we do and achieve. For me, it's the fact that I am there. I am in their midst, and I come back day after day after day. The prison visitor sits and listens, and that's a new experience for some. Through the power of listening, prisoners feel cared for and loved, maybe for the first time. They may never have been listened to by their parents or by their teachers.

Through the power of listening, prisoners feel cared for and loved, maybe for the first time.

A few years ago, while working with young offenders, I wrote a song called 'The Little Boy Inside'. I wanted to reflect on what it was like for a young offender. It's about the little boy who's crying out for mercy. He's crying out for love from inside his troubled life. On the outside is someone who's chucking stones, stabbing people and taking drugs. That's all you can see on the outside. There's a challenge in the song where he says, 'I'm waiting to be filled with some kind of light.' Maybe that light can come from you. How? Through your prayers.

If you're not involved in prison ministry as such, please pray for prisoners and their needs, and for those of us who work in prisons: chaplains and prison staff. Pray for their emotional, spiritual and physical needs. Pray for those also who work with those who are coming out of prisons. We need your prayers. It is through prayer that we change and that others can experience change. It is through prayer that we find the hope that comes from a relationship with a God of unconditional love.

— — — — — — — — — — —

Ashley's song: The Little Boy Inside
Don't be quick to judge me
Don't be swift to sneer
I'm on the rocks
And you don't kick a man when he's down
Don't be harsh and heartless
See where I come from
You may decide that I'm not that kind of man

I've been lost
I've been broken
I've been down the road to hell
It's not my fault that I was born into
The road that's on the other side of town

I'm crying out for mercy
And I'm crying out for love
The love that never came when I was young
Can you not see through my actions
That I'm hurting deep inside
That I'm crying out for someone who will love
This little boy inside

My actions may be thoughtless
And my words they may be cruel
But they're coming out from a darkness in my soul
Try and see through all the madness
That there's an emptiness inside
Waiting to be filled with some kind of light
Maybe from you
With your prayers
And your love
And your hope in me
Don't give up on me
Feel my pain
And take me to your God in prayer
Don't leave me – this boy inside

He's been lost
He's been broken
He's been down the road to hell
It's not his fault that he was born into
The road that's on the other side of town

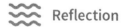 ## Reflection

- Have you ever been lost in life? How did it feel?
- We are all broken. What in you needs to be mended with love?
- How can you help those who have lost their way and are broken today?
- What is your imprisonment?

 A prayer

God of forgiveness and mercy, we thank you for the hope you offer us in the salvation of your son Jesus Christ. We pray for all those in prison, that they may know your presence and come to know the fullness of your gracious love. May we too be willing to give a second chance to those who have been lost and broken, and who wish to make a change in their lives, and find their true identity in you. We pray through Jesus Christ our Lord. Amen.

 A spiritual exercise

Prepare yourself for prayer
Sit comfortably with both feet on the ground and hands open on your lap as if waiting to receive a gift from God. Let go of your worries or thoughts and entrust yourself and everything to God. Pray that you will be receptive to what God has to say to you in this scripture reading.

Read aloud the following words from Psalm 126, slowly and meditatively. Listen for words or phrases that speak to you. Sit with it for a while.

> When the Lord restored the fortunes of Zion,
>   we were like those who dream.
> Then our mouth was filled with laughter
>   and our tongue with shouts of joy;
> then it was said among the nations,
>   'The Lord has done great things for them.'
> The Lord has done great things for us,
>   and we rejoiced.

Restore our fortunes, O Lord,
    like the watercourses in the Negeb.
May those who sow in tears
    reap with shouts of joy.
Those who go out weeping,
    bearing the seed for sowing,
shall come home with shouts of joy,
    carrying their sheaves.
PSALM 126

Meditate
Read these verses again. This time, let the words or phrases that stood out for you the first time become an invitation from God to speak with him. Allow the words to flow through you as you meditate upon them.

Pray
Now read the passage a third time, slowly.

Ask
- What is God saying to you in these words?
- What do you want to say to God?
- What feelings are stirred within you?
- Share your answers with God.

Contemplate
Read the text one last time, and this time let the words you have been praying with go free. Be still and at peace with God.

Ask
- What gift has God given you to take away?
- What action might God be inviting you to do?
- Thank God for this gift and for his invitation.

Further resources

Dietrich Bonhoeffer, *Letters and Papers from Prison*, edited by
    Samuel Wells and John Bowden (SCM Press, 2017).
Mary Brown, *Confessions of a Prison Chaplain* (Waterside, 2014).
Meins G.S. Coetsier, *Theology, Empowerment, and Prison Ministry:
    Karl Rahner and the contemporary exploration for meaning* (Brill,
    2022).
John Perry, *God Behind Bars: The inspiring story of prison fellowship*
    (Thomas Nelson, 2006).
Dennis W. Pierce, *Prison Ministry: Hope behind the wall* (Routledge,
    2006).
Jill L. Snodgrass, *Women Leaving Prison: Justice-seeking spiritual
    support for female returning citizens* (Lexington, 2018).

10

A PERFECT CADENCE?
BURYING THE DEAD

■ ■ ■ ■ ■ ■ ■ ■ ■ ■ ■ ■ ■ ■ ■ ■ ■ ■ ■ ■

> And may the music of thy name
> Refresh my soul in death.
> John Newton, New English Hymnal, hymn 374

> Sarah lived for one hundred twenty-seven years; this was the
> length of Sarah's life. And Sarah died at Kiriath-arba, that is,
> Hebron, in the land of Canaan, and Abraham went in to mourn
> for Sarah and to weep for her. Abraham rose up from beside
> his dead and said to the Hittites, 'I am a stranger and an alien
> residing among you; give me property among you for a burying
> place, so that I may bury my dead out of my sight.' The Hit-
> tites answered Abraham, 'Hear us, my lord; you are a mighty
> prince among us. Bury your dead in the choicest of our burial
> places; none of us will withhold from you any burial ground
> for burying your dead.'
> GENESIS 23:1–6

Is there such a thing as a good death, a way of bringing all the melodious themes of someone's life to a conclusion with a perfect end? In
music the end of a piece or a phrase is a cadence. As we have seen,
one such cadence can be 'interrupted' – when the music seems like it
should have lasted longer or come to a more satisfactory conclusion

or when it temporarily interrupts the flow only for the music to continue and then cadence more contently later. In our lives, conclusions or cadences can be felt as an untimely interruption of what was a beautiful story – a serious illness, a traumatising life event, a natural disaster or, more finally, a sudden or premature death. Like Schubert's 'Unfinished Symphony' (interrupted by Schubert's own death), we can feel like the death of a loved one, or those we see tragically killed by war, oppression or disaster, is a life with unfinished business, a life that could have gone on to contribute so much more to the world. Every life, however short or long, whether it ends in peaceful old age or tragically young, is equally valid and whole in the sight of God. Every baby, child and adult is a soul of equal significance and value to the creator who cherishes them.

But there is another kind of musical cadence, called the 'perfect cadence'. This is a harmonious sequence of chords that bring a sense of fulfilment, satisfaction and completion to the music. It is perhaps the most popular and conventional way to end a song or a composition. Virtually every pop song will end this way, returning, as we have heard before, to the 'home' key. In death, we too may long for this final cadence, finding the 'quiet night' and 'perfect end' to our lives, as the words of Compline put it, surrounded by loved ones, with all our affairs in order and at peace with the world and with God. I have seen such deaths and heard stories of lives which seem to have been complete and happy. My own paternal grandfather was one such man. He died in his 90s saying that he had lived a wonderful life, with no regrets and was content to reach his end.

The perfect cadence also gives us the joy of returning to the 'home' musical key, just as we may wish to feel that in our end, we are journeying home to our loving Father, in whose house there are many mansions (see John 14:2). We have heard how visiting the sick can ease the journey of the living towards death and help families come to terms with their loved one's final days. Then there is the cadence of saying goodbye, whether at a funeral or other ceremony. The traditional language of burying the dead can be part of this farewell. This work of mercy is, of course, corporeal, in that it deals with the body and what we choose to do with it once life has passed. It is practical – as well as emotional, mental and spiritual – work. It can have huge significance for the families and friends of the deceased, who is given dignity and honour in the final cadence of their days. It is an act of love that can help the process of grieving, remembering, giving thanks for a life lived, and healing, whether of wrongs forgiven or hurts mended.

Not every cadence is perfect, and we will all know many cases where contented completion is not found. Indeed, we may question whether any death can be entirely without remorse or regret.

Can we have a good death? Christ's own end was one of torment, per-secution, scourging and sacrifice, an ignominious end. But in the joy of the third day and the shock of the women at the tomb, the message rang out that the melody of Christ's mercy played on. The life that was ended by crucifixion brought new life in God. Christ's death brought salvation for humanity and for creation, through liberation. As we live in the 'now and not yet' of God's kingdom, the music plays on as angels and archangels sing God's praises, and as humanity waits for the cadence of the end times, the *eschaton*, where final judgement, justice and mercy will be delivered, and a new creation begun.

EMMA'S STORY

When I was a parish priest to three beautiful medieval churches and their equally idyllic churchyards in Oxfordshire, I used to take up to 30 funerals a year, so one of my main tasks was to bury the dead. Death and the sacred rituals which surround the end of life were a normative part of my world. The sight of a hearse driving round the village lanes in which the deceased played and lived was a regular occurrence and the folk who came to pay their last respects invariably would have at least two or three such occasions to attend each month.

But one of the images which has most haunted me over the years has been a photograph on the Médecins Sans Frontières website taken in 2015 that showed an open grave in Sierra Leone. Unlike the open graves I saw in Garsington churchyard, this one was deep and ten times as large, because it was a mass grave that held about 20 bodies, wrapped up in white shrouds lying next to each other. An aid worker stood at one end and a few people were dotted around, including a young girl, not much older than about ten. All I could think was: why was the grave still left open; why didn't they cover them over and give them peace; who was there to say the funeral service for them; where was a priest?

During the equivalent catastrophe in England during the 1340s and then again in the 1360s, the answer to that question was clear: it was the priest, the ordinary parson who carried out his duty to bury the dead. Yet of all the victims of the Black Death, it was these loyal servants of the church that suffered most, with two-thirds of them being wiped out in a matter of months. Even today, so many years later, where our worldview is radically altered, it is still the parish priest who buries the dead. A humanist minister or funeral chaplain may now have replaced the parson at the crematorium, but no one can be lowered into a grave within a churchyard without the incumbent or equivalent priest being present.

It has been commented before by those who have lived through the harrowing experience of the death of a loved one, that in the days to follow it feels as if the professionals move in, from the police who must be called out if such an incident happens at home, to the funeral director who takes them away, to the priest who comes to arrange the ceremonial. They may have a chance to see them in the chapel of rest to say goodbye, but it is these professionals who lay the last human hand on their coffin and fill in the open grave. The most a family can do in burying their loved one is to sprinkle some earth or flowers at the service. For in our modern world, burying the dead has become privatised by a series of professionals, who in the most sensitive and compassionate way help a grieving family to navigate the dark waters of burying their dead.

I guess what had so shocked me about the Médecins Sans Frontières photograph was the absence of these professionals who, in the UK, have become so necessary in the modern process of laying the dead to rest. There was no funeral director, no priest and – most telling of all – no grieving family in this picture: only a little girl and an aid worker. This picture reminded me that to bury the dead is more than just the role of the priest or the responsibility of the family; it is a work of mercy that we are all bidden to do as we live out our faith in practical and real ways.

> To bury the dead is more than just the role of the priest or the responsibility of the family; it is a work of mercy that we are all bidden to do as we live out our faith in practical and real ways.

Why is this a work of mercy?

The scriptural basis for including burying the dead within the corporeal acts of mercy can be found in the book of Tobit, one of the Apocryphal or Deuterocanonical books of the Old Testament. Tobit is probably most famous for his son Tobias, who had the archangel Raphael as his guardian angel, but Tobit, like Daniel, is an icon of a loyal Israelite who, even in captivity under the Assyrians, kept living out his faith in ordinary and practical ways. He fulfilled the corporeal acts of mercy by giving food to the hungry, clothing the naked and 'if I saw the dead body of any of my nation thrown out behind the wall of Nineveh, I would bury it' (Tobit 1:17). So he displayed the mercy of God to those he knew and did not know by ensuring that the dead were given some form of respect and burial.

The importance of proper burial can be seen in Genesis 23:1–6, which is quoted at the beginning of this chapter. Abraham, who is living among the Hittites, purchases a field in which to bury his wife Sarah, but it will also be the place where he too will be buried. Here, burial of the dead is very much a family obligation and it's the family who are going to look after and bury the dead in that place. There is also a sense of burial in a particular place as connecting and reconnecting loved ones beyond life. They will all lie together in this world as they will be reunited in the life beyond. It is a powerful idea, which lies at the heart of all funeral rituals going back to prehistoric times and has been expressed in myriad of ways throughout history and across all cultures.

Burial was considered so important in ancient Israel that being left unburied was considered a curse and a condemnation. In Deuteronomy 28, where all the curses for disobeying God's commands are listed, this curse is found: 'Your corpses will become food for all the birds of the air and for the beasts of the field, with no one to frighten them off' (v. 26, NAB). This is why, as a good Jew, Tobit is faithfully fulfilling the will of God when he says, 'If I see a dead body, even if I'm not related to that person, I will go and bury that dead person.' It becomes an act of mercy not just for your family, but to another person, even a stranger.

In the New Testament, perhaps the most famous example of burial is the deposition of Christ. It is not just Jesus' family members who wrap and anoint his body, but also the women who followed him. These women were the closest people to Jesus, acting out of love and mercy. There are several other noticeable examples in the New Testament of respectful burial by friends and followers, not just family. The body of John the Baptist, after he's been beheaded, is taken away by the disciples and buried. Similarly, after Stephen was stoned, it is noted that devout men came and buried him (Acts 8:2). I hope that none of us will find ourselves in such a desperate situation that it is down to us to physically lay the dead to rest, yet there are such people even now across the world whose task it is to do this. So how can we, in the world in which we do live, fulfil this mandate to bury the dead?

At ordination to the priesthood, one of the commands that priests are given is to 'minister to the sick and prepare the dying for their death'. This specifically looks to the care of the person before they have died or as they are dying. For many centuries this ministry by the church took the shape of the so-called last rites, which included confession, absolution, anointing and the *viaticum* or Eucharist of the dying. This is still of significance to many Christians across the world, but in the Church of England, for example, the last rites are reduced to anointing and more compassionate acts of kindness that would not need a priest. These include being able to hold the hand of the person who is dying, talking to them even when they can't speak or reading verses of scripture that reassure them that God loves them. Such ministry today is given to the person when they are alive, not when they are dead. It's a different kind of ministry to that of burying the dead.

Today the process of preparing the body for burial is mostly no longer performed by family and friends, but has become much more professionalised. There are places in the world where this is not the case, and the family are still very much involved, but here in the UK it's much more likely for the dead to be taken to a professional funeral director for preparation. This is not to say that the professionals are not performing acts of kindness, dignity and mercy in preparing the dead for burial. Embalmer Isabel Walton says, 'I don't think people realise how much care goes into the role.'[60]

There are also many different types of ways in which the loved one's body can be laid to rest. These include traditional means, such as burial (in land or at sea) or cremation; historic ways, such as mummification; and modern methods, such as a woodland burial, sky burial, chemical burial, preservation of the body through cryonics or resomation (in which water is used to break down a corpse in a kind of flame-free cremation). These are just some of the ways in which individuals rather than families can choose to dispose of their body. It is often the family who choose how to memorialise their loved one, be it through planting a tree, scattering ashes at a place the deceased loved or a plaque on a parkland bench.

Recently we have become more aware of those who die in tragic circumstances where there is no body to bury or place to mourn. At the back of the municipal cemetery in Catania, Sicily, there is a large burial ground which is dedicated to migrants who have died trying to cross the Mediterranean Sea. Each stick marks one of these 'martyrs of the sea'. The International Organization for Migration states that 24,144 people died or went missing during attempts to cross the Mediterranean between 2014 and 2023.[61] The vast majority of those deaths – 19,520 – took place in the central Mediterranean and the bodies of most of those who perished have not been recovered, according to the agency's figures. In 2022 alone 1,864 people died trying to cross the central Mediterranean.

While burial in this country has become more professionalised, the Covid-19 pandemic highlighted how horrendous and damaging it is when families are unable to attend a funeral and lay their loved ones to rest. People in protective equipment were there to try to give dignity in their death, but many today still live with the unresolved grief of not being able to undergo some form of ritual which holds grief and enables healing to begin for those left behind. There have been many pandemics in history, not least the Black Death in the 14th century, where up to 50 million are thought to have died. Other notable pandemics and epidemics include the Great Plague of 1665, where 100,000 died in London alone; the influenza pandemic of 1918, where the number of deaths globally were between 50 million and 100 million; and the 2015 Ebola crisis in some of the poorest countries in Africa, which killed around 11,500. In the UK alone, more than 225,000 died with Covid-19. Laying a loved one to rest is extremely important in order to give them dignity at the end of their life, but during a pandemic, when enormous numbers of people die , it becomes an act of mercy in which all of us are involved.

At Christmas time in Garsington, a remarkable transformation of the churchyard begins to slowly take place over the weeks leading up to this most central of all festivals, as the graves begin to be visited and covered in beautiful wreaths of flowers and candles. The sight of so many physical emblems of grief reminds everyone who walks down the path to the church that, while Christmas is a time of family and fun, for many it is a poignant reminder of loss and the empty chair that will no longer be filled. Months, even years, after a loved one has been laid in the ground, there is still the need for someone to act and speak those words of the kindness and mercy of God. The professionals soon leave; even though we would wish to be there every day to help that person through their grief, there is the next funeral to do, so it is the rest of us who must overcome our timidity and fear of saying the wrong thing to reach out to those who still need help to bury their loved ones and release them into the eternal.

So, another part of this act of mercy is to care for the grieving who have lost their loved one. The funeral service begins with lines of comfort and reassurance, which are directed not to the person who has died, but to the living. Being with people in their grief and showing little acts of kindness are how we reveal the mercy of God, caring for those who are sad and struggling and need people around in their sorrow. But here we must remember that we are but the messenger of the

Another part of this act of mercy is to care for the grieving.

mercy of God, his angel, who, through a card or a kind word, a cake or a smile, will enable someone to gradually let go into new life and help them bury their dead.

— — — — — — — — — — —

 ## Reflections

- How can we give our loved ones dignity in death as well as in life?
- How can we be merciful to the dying?
- Is death the end of our story?
- How would you like to be remembered?

 ## A prayer

Saviour Christ, you were crucified and laid in the tomb as a sacrifice for our broken world. By the redemption of your resurrection and ascension, may we with all the saints dwell with you in your eternal kingdom. Whatever our end on this earth may be, enfold us with your saving love, purge us of our human sickness and anoint us with your mercy, that we may sing your praises with the angels, and come to the perfect cadence of your new creation. Amen.

 ## A spiritual exercise

Prepare yourself for prayer
Sit comfortably with both feet on the ground and hands open on your lap as if waiting to receive a gift from God. Let go of your worries or thoughts and entrust yourself and everything to God. Pray that you will be receptive to what God has to say to you in this scripture reading.

Read the passage below out loud, slowly and meditatively. Listen for words or phrases that speak to you. Sit with it for a while.

They took the body of Jesus and wrapped it with the spices in
linen cloths, according to the burial custom of the Jews. Now
there was a garden in the place where he was crucified, and in
the garden there was a new tomb in which no one had ever been
laid. And so, because it was the Jewish day of Preparation and
the tomb was nearby, they laid Jesus there.

JOHN 19:40–42

Meditate

Read these verses again. This time, let the words or phrases that stood
out for you the first time become an invitation from God to speak with
him. Allow the words to flow through you as you meditate upon them.

Pray

Now read the passage a third time, slowly.

Ask

- What is God saying to you in these words?
- What do you want to say to God?
- What feelings are stirred within you?
- Share your answers with God.

Contemplate

Read the text one last time, and this time let the words you have been
praying with go free. Be still and at peace with God.

Ask

- What gift has God given you to take away?
- What action might God be inviting you to do?
- Thank God for this gift and for his invitation.

Further resources

Robert Atwell, *Remember: 100 readings for those in grief and bereavement* (Canterbury Press, 2005).

Laurel Dykstra (ed.), *Bury the Dead: Stories of death and dying, resistance and discipleship* (Cascade Books, 2013).

Malcolm Guite, *Love, Remember: 40 poems of loss, lament and hope* (Canterbury Press, 2017).

Peter Millar, *Finding Hope Again: Journeys through sorrow and beyond* (Canterbury Press, 2003).

Paul Sheppy, *Cries of the Heart: A daily companion for your journey through grief* (Canterbury Press, 2005).

Granger E. Westberg, *Good Grief* (SPCK, 2011).

11

COMPOSITION AND CHRIST: CARING FOR CREATION

In the beginning was the Word, and the Word was with God, and the Word was God. He was in the beginning with God. All things came into being through him, and without him not one thing came into being. What has come into being in him was life, and the life was the light of all people. The light shines in the darkness, and the darkness did not overtake it.
JOHN 1:1–5

For as the rain and the snow come down from heaven,
    and do not return there until they have watered the earth,
making it bring forth and sprout,
    giving seed to the sower and bread to the eater,
so shall my word be that goes out from my mouth;
    it shall not return to me empty,
but it shall accomplish that which I purpose
    and succeed in the thing for which I sent it.
For you shall go out in joy,
    and be led back in peace;
the mountains and the hills before you
    shall burst into song,
    and all the trees of the field shall clap their hands.
ISAIAH 55:10–12

The connection between nature and music has been a strong theme in literature throughout the ages. In the passage from Isaiah above, mountains and hills burst into song and trees make rhythmic sounds in praise of God. One way of describing music, indeed all artistic expression, is that of a creative human being offering a grateful response to the one who created us. The gift of life and all that goes with it, including artistic expression, are offered back to the creator, the composer of the universe, in thanksgiving, praise, prayer or plea. The offering is an expression of a relationship between the divine and the world, a divide that has been broken down through the self-emptying sacrifice of the incarnation of Christ, his death and resurrection.

The opening of John's gospel is a creation story – a story of creative composition of the cosmos by the divine force. Unlike Genesis, where we hear 'In the beginning God created...' (1:1, NIV), we instead hear 'In the beginning was the Word, and the Word was with God, and the Word was God. He was in the beginning with God. All things came into being through him, and without him not one thing came into being' (John 1:1–3). We may be familiar with this message, but to take it seriously is to realise that the very essence of Christ, the eternal Word, the *logos*, is woven into the fabric of our universe, and without this divine essence, nothing that exists can be sustained. This *logos* is the pre-existing song, or musical theme, that was always at the heart of our planet's reality.

In previous chapters, we have discussed the idea of polyphony (many notes sounding at the same time), an idea that can help us understand our relationship with the natural world. Christ is the song at the heart of the cosmic composition of God, the musical theme that threads through everyone and everything. In medieval music, this musical theme was called the *cantus firmus* (literally the firm or solid song), a pre-existing melody like a hymn or plainsong tune, around which other 'polyphonic' melodies could weave. This 'solid song' is at the heart of each one of us. All the many-voiced interactions

Christ is the song at the heart of the cosmic composition of God.

and relationships that we weave around it are our creative response to this divine reality at the heart of all life.

This is not a new observation. The great German theologian Jürgen Moltmann also realised that Christ is like a song in everyone and everything: 'In the quickening breath and through the form-giving word, the Creator sings out his creatures in the sounds and rhythms in which he has his joy and his good pleasure.'[62] And for Simone Weil, music, in its incarnational role, brings about harmony in humanity, just as the ancient Greek Pythagoras considered music to reflect the cosmic harmony of the spheres: 'The incarnation of Christianity implies a harmonious solution of the problem of the relations between the individual and the collective. Harmony in the Pythagorean sense: the just balance of contraries.'[63]

If Christ is the song or tune running through the heart of the cosmic composition, then we can, with Gerard Manley Hopkins, rejoice that 'the world is charged with the grandeur of God'.[64] But we must also recognise that human ecology cannot be separated from environmental ecology, for we are all interrelated. The polyphony of creation is not just played in human communities. It plays throughout the natural world. To be part of this music we must bravely feel the pain and anguish of a world where thousands of species have already become extinct because of human action, where biodiversity is being destroyed and where people flee their homes because of hostile climates. In the words of Pope Francis, 'Each creature has its own purpose. None is superfluous.'[65] It is for this reason that I include caring for creation as an extra work of mercy in this book, as if Christ is turning to us and saying, 'Just as you cared for the least created being in the world, you cared for me.' As we care for the flower, the little-known endangered species, we care for Christ. In the words of Archbishop Justin Welby, 'To live out my Christian faith is to follow Jesus. That must include standing alongside the most vulnerable and marginalized on the frontlines of the climate emergency.'[66] To stand alongside, or to 'be with' those in need is the heart of the works of mercy.

In the Bible we read that creation is holy, but also that God is liberating all creation. He is buried in earth, descends to the dead, is raised to life and ascends into heaven, as the first of a renewed creation. This is a story of salvation, a God who, from love, recreates and does not destroy humanity. We are not lifted out of the world to a spiritual realm to escape. Rather, we are remade for a renewed earth. In the gospels Jesus recreates by healing the sick, stilling storms and bringing justice out of discord. If we are to work mercy in our own world, we must engage in contemplative social action. As Pope Francis has said, we must 'become painfully aware, to dare to turn what is happening to the world into our own personal suffering and thus to discover what each of us can do about it'.[67] In our contemplative and grateful response to the gift of life, we pass the world on to the future, committing ourselves to the gospel of Jesus – the eternal *logos* who is at the heart of creation and its redemption.

So how do we take up this commitment? We commit to the mission of climate action. Climate action and care for the environment are both God's and our mission. They are about 'tuning in' to the solid song, the *cantus firmus*, of Christ, resonating in everything. This missional 'tuning in' is about finding what God is already doing and joining in, as God is actively working in creation.

Our relationship with the created world cannot, therefore, be detached from our faith. On the contrary, our theological response to our environment is at the heart of the gospel and of our faith. For Christ is the essence of all creation, and his redemption is for the whole of that creation. The story of our salvation is the story of God's work in and through his creation, a God who creates and recreates: 'See, I am making all things new', says the Lord (Revelation 21:5). God invites us to join in his work, the *missio Dei*, and to live life in all its fullness, a life where all creation is orientated towards the praise of God, where all created beings recognise our interconnectedness and joint responsibility.

Addressing the environment and climate emergency crisis requires us to understand how our environment works and the consequences of our various actions, so that we are equipped to act with commitment and make lasting changes. Ultimately, our environmental actions to care for creation and meet net-zero carbon emissions involve our radical commitment to change the way we think and act in God's world and among all his creatures. As Christians, we pray for the courage to act imaginatively, compassionately and with empathy for creation, in the knowledge that the eternal *logos*, Christ, is at the heart of creation and the redemption of the world.

The Anglican Communion's Five Marks of Mission encourage us to proclaim the good news; to teach, baptise and nurture new believers; to respond to human need by loving service; to transform unjust structures of society, to challenge violence of every kind and pursue peace and reconciliation; and to strive to safeguard the integrity of creation, and sustain and renew the life of the earth.[68] But it is not just the last of these that relates to our environment. With Christ's divine essence at the heart of creation, all these areas of mission are affected by how we respond to, and care for, our environment – and how we now act on the devastating consequences of climate change.

What can we practically do? As people of God, we must commit to learn the facts about today's environmental degradation and human-induced climate change; to speak the truth about the emergency and the changes that are needed to safeguard the environment and mitigate climate impact; to take the necessary action to reduce greenhouse gas emissions to net zero; to model ways in which our faith and congregations can enable all of God's creation to flourish; and to fight social injustices caused by the environmental crisis.

We must also take heart and act. Be grateful for the beauty and bounty of creation, freely given by a generous God; be creative in our ideas and conversations; be compassionate through acts of love and mercy for the whole of creation; be courageous in our proclamation of the gospel of justice. We must pray for world leaders and those with influence; listen and watch for God's action and join in, building communities and churches with climate action at the heart of our mission and purpose.

In their booklet on climate action and mission, Grace Thomas and Mark Coleman write of the need for both practical and prophetic action: 'Both strands of climate action, practical and prophetic, are missional in a holistic sense. They are faithful ways of working towards the kingdom of God here on Earth.'[69] In these words, we see that prayer and prophetic action are not separate parts of our faith, but closely linked. Prayer leads to solidarity, hope and love, which in turn leads to justice, peace and action.

There are four ways we can do this: prayer, evangelism, generosity and reflecting on scripture. These four priorities apply not only to our faith, but also to our understanding and perception of, and relationship with, our environment.

Prayer

Prayer is creative. By listening to and conversing with God through a personal relationship of faith and love, we are enabled to prayerfully listen to, and learn from, those who speak truth to power about climate change, and to challenge our MPs, policy makers and legislators. Through prayer and contemplation of God's word, we can become powerful prophets for change. Contemplative and reflective prayer can lead us to share in the work of climate change by creative conversations with everyone from the poorest to the richest, the weakest to the most powerful. If we are to act aright, we need to walk closely with God as our guide through prayer.

Evangelism

Jesus says, 'You are the salt of the earth' (Matthew 5:13). What marks us out as disciples of Christ is the effect we have, like salt, yeast or light – in other words, how we think, love and act. It was C.S. Lewis who wrote: 'I believe in Christianity as I believe that the sun has risen – not because I see it, but because by it I see everything else.'[70] We know

God is at work because we see the effect. When Jesus commanded, 'Go into all the world and proclaim the good news to the whole creation' (Mark 16:15), we are bidden to join in with the work of God, the *missio Dei*, and open the amazing possibilities of God's mission and work in the world.

Generosity

'Truly I tell you, just as you did it to one of the least of these brothers and sisters of mine, you did it to me' (Matthew 25:40). Climate action is a work of love and compassion for our world, for future generations and for the poorest in our societies. Every day, people are being forced from their homes because of uninhabitable or infertile environments due to climate change. Social deprivations can be caused by climate change. Therefore, our acts of love for our neighbour, as commanded by scripture, are both to care for those affected by the consequences of climate change and to generously take steps (with our time, money, attention, skill and choices) to reduce carbon emissions and to encourage other individuals, organisations and governments to do the same.

Reflecting on scripture

To proclaim God's love prayerfully and generously for creation, we will need what John Stott called 'double listening' – listening to the gospel and to the environment around us.[71] This means, in the words of Paul, that we need to be 'transformed by the renewing of the mind' (Romans 12:2). We cannot act until we have listened to God's words, prayerfully meditated upon his will, and allow him to transform our minds and hearts to serve God's mission. By doing so, we let the gospel speak into one of the most pressing and important subjects of our time.

By prayer, evangelism, generosity and reflecting on scripture, we can abide in, and tune in to, the song of Jesus. From this singing with Christ, we are given the inspiration, energy and direction to advocate and act wisely. Exactly what prophetic action we take will depend on where the Holy Spirit leads us. Each one of us will have different gifts to offer, but together we can work in greater solidarity with each other, with renewed hope and with justice, helping to change our lives and actions and bring about a better future for the planet.

We have looked at some possible ways we can respond as individuals, and as churches we continue to be creative in our ideas and conversations around climate change; be compassionate in our acts of love and mercy for the whole of creation; and be courageous in our proclamation of the gospel of justice, especially for those who have lost homes, land and family due to climate change. Climate activists and priests Thomas and Coleman have a list of suggested contemplative actions to take:

1   pray: listen and watch for God's action and join in
2   build a team: planned and supported by people with similar goals
3   engage with Eco Church (**ecochurch.arocha.org.uk**)
4   bring climate action into the parish or deanery Mission Action Plan
5   explore how you can be a prophetic voice
6   create safe spaces for grief and pastoral support, especially for the anxious and depressed about our planet
7   engage with your MP on climate issues.[72]

Teresa is an environmental specialist who has worked on marine and terrestrial conservation for years. She was the Canterbury diocesan environmental officer from 2017 to 2022, and here is a small part of her story.

TERESA'S STORY

My working life has been in the field of ecology and nature conservation. Over the years I have given much thought to the way in which we value our natural environment, the interconnectedness of all things and the importance of a healthy planet in maintaining our human existence.

For me, care for the environment comes down to caring for people. It is love for one's neighbour, love for the person that lives on the other side of the planet. For example, if people are living on low-lying land, they will be affected by sea-level rise resulting from global warming, a consequence of human actions causing climate change. So, it's about shared love and compassion, which is why the Bible passage that most speaks to me is, '"You shall love the Lord your God with all your heart and with all your soul and with all your mind." This is the great and first commandment. And a second is like it: "You shall love your neighbour as yourself"' (Matthew 22:37–39). That says it all. If I care for my neighbours, then I must care for the natural environment, because that sustains them. It's very practical.

> **Care for the environment comes down to caring for people.**

Over the billions of years that the earth was forming, the atmosphere has not always been as it is now. It has been influenced by the various species that have lived on the planet. It has changed and we've evolved. Humanity is the product of millions of years of evolution, and I suppose what makes humans special is our thinking ability or our consciousness. But also, that we are made in the image of God. If we are made in God's image, then we are made in the image of love, because God is love. It all comes back to love. Caring.

What is God doing? God is weeping. God wants us to have a greater awareness and oneness of relationship – with God and with one another – in the here and now. As I have become older, I find that it is relationships with other people that are of primary importance. How we express love for God is how we behave towards other people, and how we behave towards the environment.

If there's one thing we can do for the climate, it is to be team players, recognising what people are good at, sharing skills and abilities to tackle major issues affecting the sustainability of our natural world ecosystem, which supports our very existence. If you are caring towards the planet, then you are caring for other people. From the practical point of view, we need governments and industries to be making big changes in terms of emissions, and there is always a need for greater awareness of the facts about human-induced climate change. We also need to grow in terms of renewable energy as well as in terms of sustainability. And we need to recognise the connection between the climate and health. If we want people to be healthier, we need to look after the environment so that people don't get diseases because of poor environmental conditions. All these matters need to be addressed on a global level.

— — — — — — — — — — —

 ## Reflection

- How does climate change make you feel?
- How can you build a team to help care for the environment where you live?
- Can you write to your MP on any environmental matter?
- What is your prayer for our planet?

 ## A prayer

Creative God, we wonder at the beauty and complexity of the cosmos. We rejoice that we are fearfully and wonderfully made in your image. My Christ, the eternal logos, inspire and energise us all to work in solidarity with one another, to care for the creation entrusted to us, so that future generations may live to praise you for the gift you have given us in life. May we tune in to the cantus firmus *of your eternal love and respond imaginatively and empathetically with our polyphony of praise. Amen.*

 **A spiritual exercise**

Prepare yourself for prayer
Sit comfortably with both feet on the ground and hands open on your lap as if waiting to receive a gift from God. Let go of your worries or thoughts and entrust yourself and everything to God. Pray that you will be receptive to what God has to say to you in this scripture reading.

Read the passage below out loud, slowly and meditatively. Listen for words or phrases that speak to you. Sit with it for a while.

> For the creation waits with eager longing for the revealing of the sons of God. For the creation was subjected to futility, not willingly, but because of him who subjected it, in hope that the creation itself will be set free from its bondage to corruption and obtain the freedom of the glory of the children of God. For we know that the whole creation has been groaning together in the pains of childbirth until now. And not only the creation, but we ourselves, who have the firstfruits of the Spirit, groan inwardly as we wait eagerly for adoption as sons, the redemption of our bodies.
> ROMANS 8:19–23 (ESV)

Meditate
Read these verses again. This time, let the words or phrases that stood out for you the first time become an invitation from God to speak with him. Allow the words to flow through you as you meditate upon them.

Pray
Now read the passage a third time, slowly.

Ask
- What is God saying to you in these words?
- What do you want to say to God?

- What feelings are stirred within you?
- Share your answers with God.

Contemplate
Read the text one last time, and this time let the words you have been praying with go free. Be still and at peace with God.

Ask
- What gift has God given you to take away?
- What action might God be inviting you to undertake?
- Thank God for this gift and for his invitation.

Further reading and websites

Michael Abbaté, *Gardening Eden: How creation care will change your faith, your life, and our world* (Waterbrook Press, 2009).

Jim Antal, *Climate Church, Climate World: How people of faith must work for change* (Rowman and Littlefield, 2018).

Margaret Barker, *Creation: A biblical vision for the environment* (T&T Clark, 2010).

Kathryn D. Blanchard and Kevin J. O'Brien, *An Introduction to Christian Environmentalism: Ecology, virtue, and ethics* (Baylor University Press, 2014).

Christian Aid, 'Song of the Prophets: A global theology of climate change', November 2014, **sodorandman.im/wp-content/uploads/2021/04/song-of-prophets-global-theology-climate-change-november-2014.pdf**

John Chryssavgis, *Creation as Sacrament: Reflections on ecology and spirituality* (T&T Clark, 2019).

Diocese of Canterbury, 'Why care?', **canterburydiocese.org/mission/caring-for-creation/why-care**

Denis Edwards, *Deep Incarnation: God's redemptive suffering with creatures* (Orbis Books, 2019).

Robert McKim (ed.), *Laudato Si' and the Environment: Pope Francis' green encyclical* (Routledge, 2019).
Ruth Valerio, *Saying Yes to Life* (SPCK, 2019).
Norman Wirzba, *From Nature to Creation: A Christian vision for understanding and loving our world* (Baker Academic, 2015).

CONCLUSION

And, finally, I know, I know with all my being, with all my faith, with all the spiritual force granted to the human soul, that at this moment God is visiting this world. And the world can receive that visit, open its heart… and then in an instant our temporary and fallen life will unite with the depths of eternity.

Mother Maria Skobtsova[73]

When he came to Nazareth, where he had been brought up, he went to the synagogue on the Sabbath day, as was his custom. He stood up to read, and the scroll of the prophet Isaiah was given to him. He unrolled the scroll and found the place where it was written:

'The Spirit of the Lord is upon me,
    because he has anointed me
        to bring good news to the poor.
He has sent me to proclaim release to the captives
    and recovery of sight to the blind,
        to let the oppressed go free,
to proclaim the year of the Lord's favour.'

And he rolled up the scroll, gave it back to the attendant, and sat down. The eyes of all in the synagogue were fixed on him. Then he began to say to them, 'Today this scripture has been fulfilled in your hearing.' All spoke well of him and were amazed at the gracious words that came from his mouth. They said, 'Is not this Joseph's son?' He said to them, 'Doubtless you will quote to me this proverb, "Doctor, cure yourself!" And you will say, "Do here also in your hometown the things that we have heard you did at Capernaum."' And he said, 'Truly I tell you, no prophet is accepted in his hometown. But the truth is, there were many widows in Israel in the time of Elijah, when the heaven was shut up for three years and six months and there was a severe famine over all the land, yet Elijah was sent to none of them except to a widow at Zarephath in Sidon. There were also many with a skin disease in Israel in the time of the prophet Elisha, and none of them was cleansed except Naaman the Syrian.' When they heard this, all in the synagogue were filled with rage. They got up, drove him out of the town, and led him to the brow of the hill on which their town was built, so that they might hurl him off the cliff. But he passed through the midst of them and went on his way.

LUKE 4:16–30

My friend Andy has given me a picture. It is a pen sketch drawn while he was in Canterbury Cathedral listening to the beautiful music of Gabriel Fauré's 'Requiem', in which I took part. The sketch depicts the musicians in the choir stalls and the conductor.

I didn't receive this picture until some weeks after the event. He left it for me in the cathedral offices, and after being put in several different pigeonholes it found its way to me. David, the director of music, handed it to me one day, saying, 'Do you know anything about this?' 'Oh yes!' I replied, 'That's from Andy. He comes to the community meal on a Tuesday in Ramsgate.' It's a meal where anyone is welcome and tends to be popular with the homeless and vulnerable. There are sometimes guests who are the worse for wear, from drink or drugs, and sometimes they have grievances with each other, which can lead to the odd altercation. But mostly it's a friendly group of people from many walks of life, enjoying food together.

I have been known to try to 'entertain' the 50 or so gathered at the meal with some terrible piano playing – usually old favourites like 'Daisy Daisy', or songs by The Beatles. Sometimes I am accompanied by Dora, one of the guests who sings and sometimes dances, and Martin, who plays the harmonica.

I turn over the pen sketch and I see some writing: 'For Jonathan ? [surname unknown] Lay clerk and soloist from Andrew at King's Hill George's Meal! p.s. Thank God you're a better singer than a piano player!' It makes me chuckle.

Andy's gentle mockery and our connection with the meal, as well as our joint enjoyment of music in a cathedral, reminds me of our shared experiences of sharing food, time, music, food and laughter with one another. I am grateful for the gift and for the accurate critique of my musical skills!

But it also reminds me that in any relationship there is power. Between boss and employee, ruler and ruled, rich and poor, educated and uneducated, husband and wife, partner and partner, friend and friend. Christians are often uncomfortable talking about power. But to ignore it is to miss the opportunity of intentionally making every moment a time when each one of us can use our skills, knowledge, money and time wisely, compassionately and fairly. And if we are on the receiving end of someone else's use of power, be it benefaction, blessing, discipline, care or indeed art, we can acknowledge that the works of mercy and social justice involve the right use of power. Whether it is social policy, finance or legislation, or whether it is simple acts of individual kindness. The works of mercy as set out in Matthew 25:35–40 are not simply 'doing to' actions. Each of them is the fruit of Christ's own modelling of the good human life, a life that is incarnational, embedded in community and suffering, the coming alongside of one person to another for mutual flourishing – where the barriers between the so-called beneficiary and benefactor break down as we learn to live with and for one another.

Social justice is not about 'us' and 'them', the haves and the have-nots. In the communal life, if one suffers, we all suffer. As we saw in chapter 2, the Swahili idea of *Ubuntu* means 'I am because we are.' Without the 'we' there is no 'I'. Identity, fulfilment, growth, happiness and learning happen when the individual recognises their need of, and contribution to, the whole – other people, nature, our environment, God. Without communal reciprocal giving, with mind, heart and soul, there can be no love. Love is the beginning and the ending of our existence. To practise self-giving each day, in our own callings and as much as we are able, is to play our part in incarnating the gospel imperative for love, mercy and justice, in the everyday values of the kingdom that is to come.

The everyday God

The everyday God is a God who is visible through his works and actions every day, and is a God who is for everyone, rich or poor, privileged or lowly, addicted or clean, intellectual or uneducated. The everyday God appears in everyday events and ordinary people, and often is manifest in the most unexpected or seemingly unlikely places. He calls us to move out of our comfort zones and into his liminal space on the margins of our society, to see the face of Christ in a stranger, whose language and culture we do not know, and who yet brings us grace and blessings from afar. Or we see the everyday God in the progress of a young man released from prison who is given a chance of a home and a life away from crime. We feel the everyday God in the joy and free-dom of singing together old familiar songs and laughing in friendship with those living with dementia. And we see the everyday God in a home-less refugee who, like Jesus himself, had no home, having fled persecution.

> The everyday God appears in everyday events and ordinary people, and often is manifest in the most unexpected or seemingly unlikely places.

In the works of mercy, we not only tune in to God and God's mission, we also participate in the music of Christ's mercy, as Stanley Hauerwas reminds us:

> The purpose of the polyphony of Christ is to call humanity into participative performance with the melodies of the divine being made known in the world. It is a call to discipleship, because we worship a God who is pure act, an eternally performing God.[74]

God is active in the world. This participation relieves us of the illusion that we are instigating the work of God ourselves. However we respond to the work of God in and through the works of mercy, we are only ever tuning in and joining in with the 'polyphony of God in Christ'.[75] So, we never do these works of mercy alone, for we are part of the harmony of God's evolving creation and recreation, united with the eternal music of the Trinity. This is why, in resonance with this harmony, we are always stronger in community and when we do things together. God is composer, performer and recreator of all that is. If we listen seriously to God's melody, and tune in, we hear it everywhere, and in the everyday, and in everyone.

When we obey the greatest commands – to love our God and love our neighbour – and enter fully into the relationships that both of those acts involve, then there is no limit to what can be achieved.

CODA: MY STORY

This coda is a story about music, social justice, well-being and spirituality. It is a personal journey of discovery concerning the ethics, social benefits and spiritual nature of community. The journey is physical as well as psychological and spiritual; it is personal as well as communal; it is circumstantial, and yet it is about ethical, spiritual and compassionate concerns, arising from a natural response to human need and informed by experience of music's powers of social cohesion, physical and mental well-being, and spiritual nourishment.

In February 2019, our family moved to Canterbury, where my wife, Emma, had been offered the position of canon missioner at Canterbury Cathedral. Having settled the children into their new school and ourselves into our house, I spent the next six months finishing my role back in Oxford, during which time I looked ahead and knew that I needed a new post closer to the family in Canterbury. By fate or providence, one came up: 'director of communities and partnerships in the diocese of Canterbury'. I was not exactly sure what this role entailed, but it turned out to be the department, or 'framework' engaged in community outreach, that responded to the poorest, most vulnerable and marginalised people in our society, as well as the needs of our environment.

I applied for and was offered the role, and began in September 2019. I learned about the portfolio of projects that evolve in response to times of crises, including migration and refugees, social issues of debt, hunger, homelessness, modern slavery and exploitation, the rehabilitation of ex-offenders and rural justice. I learned about the team's range of expertise, as well as being linked into a wider network of diverse, knowledgeable and passionate people. It seemed far removed from my former work, taking me at times well beyond the borders of my comfort zones. But instinctively I became aware of the transformative power of relationships and community as we, as a team, drew alongside those in desperate need.

Many exciting new opportunities and projects emerged as we moved into 2020, but as a musician and a theologian, I wondered how music could play a part in the spiritual lives of those engaging with our work. How could we relate through music and how could music help the homeless, the mentally and physically vulnerable, the refugee and asylum seeker? How could music help us understand our need to take urgent action on climate change? And perhaps a more fundamental question remained: why bring music into this work of social justice and social care at all? What is the evidence to suggest it could have something to offer?

It seemed to me that music must play a significant role in the 'communities and partnerships' work of the diocese. And I was not alone in thinking so. I soon met a kindred spirit, a musician who has a passion for music and well-being: Adrian Bawtree.

Adrian Bawtree was acting assistant organist of Canterbury Cathedral and is now director of music at Rochester Cathedral. He is a composer, choir director, accompanist and much besides. Although we had trained at the same institutions, we had never met before, but we soon realised that our ideas concerning music's transformative power had much in common. Together we began to explore how music can help transform society and individuals through its power to inspire, heal and galvanise social cohesion and action. As we got to know each other, we drew upon our experience of community engagement through music and the arts and started to think about how the biblical imperative to love one's neighbour through practical and applied theology is evident through our experience of the gift of music. As a result, projects with the homeless, refugees, the poor and marginalised, as well as those suffering from dementia, are just some of the contexts in which we have sought to bring the gift of music into the realm of social justice, with inspiring results.

One project that had begun before lockdown, in early 2020, was Friendly Singing, an activity for older people and their carers, supported by the Friends of Canterbury Cathedral. Initially, the event was held weekly in St Paul's Church Hall in Canterbury. Each session involved a wholly inclusive and welcoming atmosphere of fun, singing a mixture of folk and classic songs, such as 'My bonny lies over the ocean', 'Early one morning', 'Can't help falling in love with you', 'A nightingale sang in Berkeley Square', with words printed in large type on a single double-sided sheet. In the first week around 20 people participated. Adrian's style is relaxed, informal, light-hearted with plenty of jokes and anecdotes along the way but led with musical skill. A recurring feature of the sessions is laughter.

Adrian's knowledge and experience of singing technique and choir training were clear, but it was also important that this was not a *choir* and no specific standards were required, only a willingness for people to have a go and have fun. By the second week, numbers had already doubled to around 40, but by February 2020 Covid was beginning to make itself evident, and conversations about stopping social gatherings, especially those involving the elderly and vulnerable, were underway.

Thus, from a promising start, the venture came to an abrupt halt in March 2020. And the question arose as to what we could do to carry the momentum forwards. Adrian suggested to the Friends of Canterbury Cathedral that he continue to produce online resources that could be used at home or played in care homes, so that people could attend virtually and sing in safety.

Adrian started putting videos together. Each episode was complete with text, soft background music to accompany any speaking, and edited visual aids, pictures and guest appearances. Each video, lasting around 20 minutes, began with a brief warm-up, with Adrian at the piano, and an introduction to the songs. As each song was played the words would appear on the screen. Usually there would be a singer, either myself, Adrian's wife Victoria or another professional, to end the show with a rendition of something familiar, such as 'Oh, what a beautiful morning!' from *Oklahoma!*, 'The White Cliffs of Dover', or Elvis Presley's 'Can't help falling in love', sung by our friend Greg dressed in full Elvis costume! A special Christmas edition appeared with several of us singing well-known Christmas songs, sat around log fires or Christmas trees. Often, Adrian would also include a hymn or two played on the cathedral organ, in the knowledge that many people would know familiar old hymns.[76]

The films were advertised, with YouTube links, through the regular emailing of the Friends of Canterbury Cathedral to thousands of people. The videos were also sent to care homes, which had closed their doors to visitors.

The extreme changes to our society because of Covid-19 and the lockdowns brought many challenges to community engagement and social justice, much of which relies on social and pastoral contact. The crisis highlighted the many ways in which parish and community engagement with social justice and care for the vulnerable have blossomed. Innumerable imaginative and responsive initiatives have been set up, which have demonstrated the enormous desire and ability of our communities to care for those locally in most need. By so doing, a mutual learning and joint ministry has flourished, whereby those who minister to others are thereby ministered to. In helping, one is helped. We have learned much from months of lockdown and we have an opportunity now to discern the work of the future and to adapt our ways to it.

Since these days of lockdown, 'communities and partnerships' has become The Social Justice Network, a registered charity owned by the diocese and still working with those most in need.

God has been active and taken me, and others, on a journey of discovery. I may have begun the role in 2019 with trepidation and more than a little ignorance of the challenges ahead, and I have been pushed into many situations that I would never have thought I would experience. My comfort zones are now much wider and more numerous, my experience of humanity is broader, my empathy is deeper, my anger at injustice fiercer, my patience with authoritarian incompetence and lack of compassion shorter. Making music, whether professionally or with friends, is not only the antidote to the stress and distress of our broken society, but it is also the symbiotic partner to the works of mercy. It is a gift of God that soothes and satisfies, but it also reminds me every day, in the words which we sing in Mary's Magnificat, 'He hath put down the mighty from their seat, and hath exalted the humble and meek.' This is the vision that the everyday God demands from his children. Every time I sing this vision, I am once again in tune with our inspiring, creative, merciful and just everyday God.

APPENDIX 1: STORYTELLERS AND MUSIC MAKERS

Nick Ash: Revd Nick Ash is a chaplain at a prison in the south of England.

Adrian Bawtree: Adrian is an English composer and organist who currently serves as director of music and organist at Rochester Cathedral.

Martin Burrell: Revd Martin Burrell is bishop's advisor for Gypsy, Romany and Traveller (GTR) communities in the diocese of Canterbury and author of two books on ministry with GTR communities.

Julia Burton-Jones: As well as being Anna Chaplaincy lead for Rochester and Canterbury Dioceses, Julia is training and development lead with the national Anna Chaplaincy team at BRF Ministries.

Patrick Ellisdon: Revd Patrick Ellisdon is vicar of All Saints Church in Canterbury. He is the former vicar of St Paul's Church, Cliftonville and co-project leader, with his wife Debbie Ellisdon, for the Canterbury diocesan project Ignite. Together they oversee projects planted through the diocese to extend the concept of Ignite to people who are not engaging with normal mainstream church, especially those who are social disadvantaged.

Dominic Fenton: Revd Dominic Fenton is rector of Holy Trinity Church, Broadstairs in Kent and was, for over 14 years the trust lead and senior chaplain at the North Middlesex University Hospital NHS Trust in Enfield in Middlesex, Edmonton. He is also a former precentor of Westminster Abbey.

Sharon Goodyer: Sharon is the founder of Our Kitchen and other food initiatives that have helped thousands of people with affordable food in Thanet, Kent.

Matthew Hergest: Matthew is a retired trader from the city of London. He ran the weekly community meal at St George's Parish Hall in Ramsgate.

Chris Maclean: Revd Chris Maclean was vicar of the Romney Marsh Benefice with 14 parish churches on a long flat parish along the coastline in East Kent.

Bradon Muilenburg: Bradon is the Anglican refugee support lead in Calais, and funded by the diocese of Europe, diocese of Canterbury and the United Society for the Propagation of the Gospel (USPG).

Kelly Napier: Kelly is director of CampaignKent CIC, which advocates for social change and provides services for the homeless in Kent. She is also manager of the Break the Cycle Project, which provides supported accommodation to prison leavers who would otherwise be homeless.

Helen Netherton: Helen runs Connecting Canterbury, which helps poor and vulnerable people with small energy grants, funds for essential house items and credit union accounts, as well as finance, food and debt advice at community hubs.

Domenica Pecoraro: Domenica is the Kent refugee programmes manager for the diocese of Canterbury.

Emma Pennington: Revd Dr Emma Pennington is canon missioner of Canterbury Cathedral and former parish priest in the diocese of Oxford.

Teresa Redfern: Teresa is a qualified ecologist and environmental scientist. She has worked on nature conservation projects across Great Britain. From 2017 to 2022 she was the Canterbury diocesan environmental officer.

Kirrilee Reid: Revd Kirrilee Reid is chaplain of the Bield at Blackruthven Retreat and Conference Centre, in Perth, Scotland, and former refugee project officer in Calais (for dioceses of Europe, Canterbury and USPG).

Jo Richards: Revd Canon Jo Richards is rector of the parish of St Dunstan's, St Mildred's and St Peter's in Canterbury town centre and area dean. She is chaplain to the homeless in Canterbury and an honorary canon of Canterbury Cathedral.

Elizabeth Rooke: Liz Rooke is a retired headteacher and runs the community larder at All Saints' Church in Canterbury.

David Slater: Canon David Slater is bishop's chaplain for workplace mission in the diocese of Canterbury, coordinating chaplain for Dover and Shepway Kent Critical Incidents across Kent, and chaplain at the Port of Dover and Eurotunnel. He gives a coastal perspective on the migrant situation and the effects it has on those already in the UK. He is an honorary canon of Canterbury Cathedral.

APPENDIX 2: SOUNDBITES

We have heard some moving and hopefully inspiring stories in this book and reflected upon them. In these economically, socially and environmentally troubling times, here are a few short soundbites about what the work of the Social Justice Network (SJN) means to people, both from within and outside the charity. They express a little of the motivation, passion and dedication that people give in times of need, poverty, homelessness, global migration and global warming. These comments also highlight that, in addition to the 'constructive justice' of our political and legal systems, we need 'corrective justice'. And how we find the strength to persist in this practice of corrective, or social, justice, because we are participating in with a work already begun by God, the music of the mission of Christ's melody of mercy.

> There may be some interesting moments but it is a privilege to serve in the community and to see the grace and mercy of God in action. What may not seem much to many is actually everything to someone else… The work of the SJN is so wide and varied, it's great to be part of the team and support each other to make a difference in the diocese of Canterbury.
> Helen Netherton

The question Jesus was once challenged with about why he chose to eat with tax collectors and sinners elicited the response, 'It is not the healthy who need a doctor, but the sick. I have not come to call the righteous, but sinners to repentance.' Prison chaplaincy is about being with the sick of society. It's about listening to the people society wants to forget. It's about giving these people a sense that someone cares enough to listen to their needs. And it's through this demonstration of God's love and care for those deemed to be sinners and outcasts that true transformation can and does happen.

Nick Ash

When I chat with the Roma women who I meet begging on the corners of all the big towns and cities of Europe, I remind myself that it was to such as these that Jesus spoke when he wandered around the streets in his day. And I pray quietly in my heart: 'May I see in the faces of these outcasts of today's society the face of Jesus himself.'

Martin Burrell

Working alongside those seeking safety broadens one horizon. Global issues such as war, famine and injustice cross oceans and arrive to our doorstep. It's our choice to respond or not as citizens. However, it is our responsibility as Christians to act as Jesus would. The SJN is a vibrant place to serve, and we are only meant to grow further tackling issues at the root of injustice wherever present in our communities, one person at the time.

Domenica Pecoraro

Alongside running my own business over the years, it has been a burden on my heart to help others. So from 2000 to 2015, I organised an annual charity concert to do fundraising for various charities. The lord mayor of Canterbury would be invited, and it was a big family outing. Musicians and singers came from all over the south-east of England and participated freely with no fees. We raised thousands of pounds for charities, such as Kent MS Therapy Centre, CLIC Sergent, Kent Kids Miles of Smiles and Catching Lives, among others. Since 2015, I have been doing volunteer fundraising for various charities in and around Canterbury. I heartily recommend anyone interested to do their bit to help those in need.

Ralph Lombart, supporter of the All Saints' Community Larder project

SJN came from the successes of the diocese of Canterbury's recent history with social justice issues. The more nimble nature of a focussed charity enables engagement to be timely and bring a coordinated partnership approach to issues. This book explores not only what is happening as a Christian institutional response to need, but also what is possible.

Stephen Taylor, former archdeacon of Maidstone and Canterbury diocesan secretary

At this time when people struggle more than ever to meet their own and their family's needs there is great need for acts of mercy. People who are experiencing physical needs, such as hunger, lack of warm clothing or adequate shelter, cannot begin to focus on their spiritual needs until these basic needs are met. When we meet them in that need, we show them God enabling them to see Him more clearly. Jonathan in his work with the SJN does this with wisdom, humility and gentle kindness.

Debbie Ellisdon, co-founder of and current project lead for Ignite

Guests of and volunteers at the community larder and café at All Saints Church in Canterbury were asked what brings them each Friday. Here were some responses from guests:

'Socialising.'
'Meeting people and friends.'
'Eating biscuits.'
'Company and chit chat.'
'Kindness of people.'
'Friendly staff.'
'Supportive environment.'
'Non judgmental attitudes.'
'Warmest welcome possible.'
'Food is very helpful.'
'Getting other help I need.'
'Generosity of volunteers.'

The following were from volunteers:

'Time for me to give back a little in life.'
'Wonderful friends and people's generosity.'
'I enjoy helping people and chatting with them.'
'Having wonderful people leading us and guiding us on what is needed.'
'Socialising.'
'Kindness and generosity.'
'Seeing the larder full of "nice items" so we can give something to the community.'
'Joy on the faces of those distributing food.'
'The chance to learn more about the local community and its needs.'
'Coming together with a variety of people and working as a team.'
'Learning different tasks every week!'
'Trying to respond to the call "to do justice, love kindness and walk humbly with God".'
'Giving a smile, a chat or a hug to make a difference to someone's day.'
'The opportunity to serve the community; to help people in need; to be part of a supportive and diverse team; to be able to encourage others; and for the privilege of hearing the stories of people's lives and to learn from them.'

NOTES

1 Craig Gardiner, *Melodies of New Monasticism: Bonhoeffer's vision, Iona's witness* (SCM, 2018), p. 52.
2 Gardiner, *Melodies of New Monasticism*, p. 72.
3 Kevin J. Vanhoozer, 'What is everyday theology? How and why Christians should read culture', in Kevin J. Vanhoozer, Charles A. Anderson and Michael J. Sleasman (eds), *Everyday Theology: How to read cultural texts and interpret trends* (Baker, 2007), p. 17, quoted in Benjamin Kautzer, 'The works of mercy: towards a liturgical ethic of the everyday', unpublished doctoral thesis, University of Durham (2015), p. 1.
4 Paul Tillich, *Systematic Theology*, volume 1 (University of Chicago Press, 1951), p. 235.
5 St John of the Cross, *San Juan de la Cruz: Dichos de luz y amor* [*Saint John of the Cross: meditative works*], translated by Terence O'Reilly (Iona, 2022), p. 64; Thomas Aquinas, *Summa Theologiae*, II-II.30.1.
6 Bernard of Clairvaux, 'Sermons on the Song of Songs', 61:3–5, quoted in 'Bernard of Clairvaux: My merit comes from his mercy', **enlargingtheheart.wordpress.com/2010/01/27/bernard-of-clairvaux-my-merit-comes-from-his-mercy**
7 Quoted in Brian Kolodiejchuk, 'Mercy and Mother Teresa', *Omnes*, 4 April 2016, **omnesmag.com/en/newsroom/la-misericordia-and-mother-teresa**
8 Rule of Benedict 53:1, citing Matthew 25:35.
9 Rule of Benedict 36:1, 5–6.
10 Rule of Benedict 4:14–21.
11 Pope Francis, 'The Angelus', Saint Peter's Square, 8 December 2015.
12 Maria Skobtsova, *Essential Writings* (Orbis, 2003), p. 119.
13 W.T. Flynn, '"The soul is symphonic": meditation of Luke 15:25 and Hildegard of Bingen's Letter 23', in D. Zager (ed.), *Music and Theology: Essays in honor of Robin A. Leaver* (Scarecrow Press, 2007), p. 2.

14 St Ignatius of Antioch, 'Epistle to the Ephesians', in Maxwell Staniforth (trans.), *Early Christian Writings: The Apostolic Fathers* (Penguin, 1987), p. 62.

15 Flynn, 'The soul is symphonic', p. 2.

16 Flynn, 'The soul is symphonic', pp. 4–5.

17 Ed Vulliamy, 'Bridging the gap, part two', *The Guardian*, 13 July 2008.

18 Martin Charlesworth and Natalie Williams, *The Myth of the Undeserving Poor: A Christian response to poverty in Britain today* (Grosvenor House, 2014), p. 68.

19 Paul Tillich, *The Shaking of the Foundations* (Penguin, 1962), p. 60.

20 Karl Rahner, 'The Eucharist and our daily lives', in *Theological Investigations, Volume 7: Further theology of the spiritual life I*, trans. David J. Bourke (Darton, Longman and Todd, 1971), p. 226.

21 Don Saliers, *Music and Theology* (Abingdon Press, 2007), p. 44.

22 Walter Brueggemann, *Israel's Praise: Doxology against idolatry and ideology* (Fortress Press, 1988), pp. 85–86.

23 James H. Cone, *The Spirituals and the Blues* (Orbis, 1972), ch. 2.

24 St Ambrose cited in *Populorum Progressio*, encyclical of Pope Paul VI on the development of peoples, 26 March 1967, **vatican.va/content/ paul-vi/en/encyclicals/documents/hf_p-vi_enc_26031967_ populorum.html**

25 Philip Booth, 'The meaning of the common good and social justice', *Catholic Social Thought*, 21 June 2021, **catholicsocialthought.org. uk/the-meaning-of-the-common-good-and-social-justice**

26 The Salvation Army, International Social Justice Commission, *Jesus and Justice*, 2011, **salvationarmy.org.nz/sites/default/files/files/ tsmp_int_social_justice.pdf**

27 The Salvation Army, *Jesus and Justice*.

28 Gardiner, *Melodies of New Monasticism*, p. 245.

29 Charlesworth and Williams, *The Myth of the Undeserving Poor*, p. 87.

30 Samuel Wells, *Act Justly: Practices to reshape the world* (Canterbury Press, 2022), pp. 20–21.

31 Skobtsova, *Essential Writings*, p. 186.

32 David Sheppard, *Bias to the Poor* (Hodder, 1983), p. 10.

33 Sheppard, *Bias to the Poor*, p. 201.

34 Kaya Burgess, 'Britain is no longer a Christian country, say frontline clergy', *The Times*, 29 August 2023.

35 Sheppard, *Bias to the Poor*, p. 14.

36 Linda Woodhead, 'Love and justice', *Studies in Christian Ethics* 5:1 (1992), pp. 48, 56.

37   Gustavo Gutiérrez, *We Drink from Our Own Wells: The spiritual journey of a people*, trans. Matthew J. O'Connell (second edition, SCM Press, 2005), p. 104.

38   Samuel Wells, *Incarnational Ministry: Being with the church* (Canterbury Press, 2017), p. 10.

39   Wells, *Incarnational Ministry*, p. 10.

40   Wells, *Incarnational Ministry*, pp. 10–12.

41   Al Barrett and Ruth Harley, *Being Interrupted: Reimagining the church's mission from the outside, in* (SCM Press, 2020), p. 40.

42   Barrett and Harley, *Being Interrupted*, p. 54.

43   Barrett and Harley, *Being Interrupted*, pp. 125–33.

44   Barrett and Harley, *Being Interrupted*, pp. 134–36.

45   Barrett and Harley, *Being Interrupted*, pp. 77–80.

46   Samuel Wells, *A Nazareth Manifesto: Being with God* (Wiley, 2015); *Incarnational Mission: Being with the world* (Canterbury Press, 2018).

47   Jennifer Harvey, 'What would Zacchaeus do? The case for disidentifying with Jesus', in George Yancy (ed.), *Christology and Whiteness: What would Jesus do?* (Routledge, 2012), pp. 98–99 (quoted in Barrett and Harley, *Being Interrupted*, p. 83).

48   Barrett and Harley, *Being Interrupted*, p. 84.

49   Jan Pahl and Martin Vye, 'Poverty in Canterbury today', report of the Canterbury Sustainable Development Goals Forum, 2023, **canterburysociety.org.uk/about-us/projects/poverty-in-canterbury-today-a-major-report**

50   Steve Sjogren, *Conspiracy of Kindness: A unique approach to sharing the love of Jesus* (Baker, 2008).

51   See **acts435.org.uk**

52   From Transforming Lives for Good. See **tlg.org.uk/your-church/make-lunch**

53   Wells, *Incarnational Mission*, pp. 235–36.

54   Wells, *Incarnational Mission*, p. 240.

55   Desmond Tutu, *In God's Hands: The Archbishop of Canterbury's Lent book 2015* (Bloomsbury, 2014).

56   The Holy See, 'Message of His Holiness Pope Francis for the twenty-sixth World Day of the Sick 2018', 26 November 2017.

57   The Constitution of the World Health Organization. See **who.int/about/accountability/governance/constitution**

58   Bryan Stevenson, *Just Mercy: A story of justice and redemption* (Scribe, 2015), p. 126.

59   Ian Cohen, 'Visit the prisoner', sermon preached at Worcester College

Chapel, Oxford, 2015.

60 Lucy Wallis, 'The 24-year-old embalmer preparing bodies for "last goodbyes"', BBC News, 9 November 2023, **bbc.co.uk/news/uk-67344417**

61 **iom.int/data-and-research**

62 Jürgen Moltmann, *The Way of Jesus Christ: Christology in messianic dimensions* (Minneapolis, 1993), p. 289.

63 Simone Weil, *Waiting for God* (Harper Perennial, 2009), p. 77.

64 Gerald Manley Hopkins, 'God's grandeur', in *Poems and Prose* (Penguin, 1985).

65 Pope Francis, 'Encyclical Letter *Laudato Si'* of The Holy Father Francis on Care for our Common Home' (*Laudato Si'*), 24 May 2015, p. 84, **vatican.va/content/francesco/en/encyclicals/documents/papa-francesco_20150524_enciclica-laudato-si.html**

66 See **canterburydiocese.org/mission/caring-for-creation/why-care**

67 *Laudato Si'*, 19.

68 See **anglicancommunion.org/mission/marks-of-mission.aspx**

69 Grace Thomas and Mark Coleman, *Climate Action as Mission: How to link the gospel with safeguarding creation* (Grove Books, 2021), p. 8.

70 C.S. Lewis, 'They asked for a paper', in *Is Theology Poetry?* (Geoffrey Bless, 1962), p. 164.

71 John Stott, *The Contemporary Christian: An urgent plea for double listening* (IVP, 1992), p. 13.

72 Thomas and Coleman, *Climate Action as Mission*, pp. 21–24.

73 Skobtsova, *Essential Writings*, p. 139.

74 Stanley Hauerwas, *Performing the Faith: Bonhoeffer and the practice of nonviolence* (SPCK, 2004), p. 77.

75 Gardiner, *Melodies of New Monasticism*, p. 61.

76 You can watch the films on Adrian's YouTube site, **youtube.com/@adrianbawtree8603**

ACKNOWLEDGEMENTS

I would like to thank all those who have helped and encouraged the completion of this book. My sincere appreciation goes to those who have contributed in any way, especially Nick Ash, Adrian Bawtree, Martin Burrell, Julia Burton-Jones, Patrick and Debbie Ellisdon, Dominic Fenton, Andrew Feltham, Sharon Goodyer, Matthew Hergest, Chris Maclean, Bradon Muilenburg, Kelly Napier, Helen Netherton, Domenica Pecoraro, Emma Pennington, Teresa Redfern, Kirrilee Reid, Jo Richards, Elizabeth Rooke, and David Slater. I wish to thank Ghislaine Howard for allowing me to reproduce some of her beautiful works of art, and my editor at BRF Ministries, Olivia Warburton, for all her wisdom and guidance, and to Daniele Och for his excellent copy editing. I also owe an enormous debt to Jan Spurlock for her care and attention to the text and, as always, for her wise advice and counsel. Any mistakes remaining in the text are entirely my own.

I wish to express my sincere gratitude to those who have worked for the Social Justice Network (SJN) past and present, and all the many volunteers and supporters, without whom the work could not happen, especially to Karen Adams for her many years of service, as well as Karen Carolan-Evans and Rachel Target, Paul Sandham for his guidance and wisdom and to the SJN trustees, who have been so supportive and helpful: Val Wallis, Carol Smith, David Kemp, Jeremy Cross, Will Adam, Miranda Ford, Tim Woolmer, Reem Khider and, from former years, Jane Ashton, Andrew Sewell, Keith Berry, Katie Janman and Amanda Cottrell. From the Diocese of Canterbury, I have had amazing support for our work, especially from Archbishop Justin Welby, Bishop Rose Hudson-Wilkin, Stephen Taylor, Doug Gibb, and Sara

222 THE EVERYDAY GOD

Endicott-Clarke, Shoween Muir, Sarah Buchan, Phil Greig, Bob Weldon, Tina Twelves, Joyce Addison, and to Steve Coneys, who introduced me to Barrett and Harley's Being Interrupted, for which I am grateful. A big thank you to Neville Emslie, Quentin Roper, Orla Garratt, and their teams, all those who sit on Synod and Archbishop's Council, and many wonderful colleagues too numerous to mention but no less important. We have partnered with many organisations, but especially Canterbury Cathedral, and I would like to thank the canon missioner, Emma Pennington, and the dean, David Monteith, for their support, and I would particularly like to thank our partners at the Kent Refugee Action Network, especially Razia Shariff, and the Clewer (anti-slavery) Initiative, especially Caroline Virgo and Bill Crooks.

I wish to thank my parents, Brenda and Christopher, for all their unfailing love, kindness, support and guidance over the years as well as Glen, Colin, Lesley and Angie. I wish to express my heartfelt love for our children, Katie and Thomas, without whom no book would be worth writing. And of course, to companions in the journey, Smudge the cat and Flossy the dog. But most of all, to Emma, for whom words cannot express my admiration, respect, gratitude and heartfelt love. Thank you for being with me every step along the way, through joy, laughter, tears and pain, but most of all for your love.

It's never been more important to understand how much God loves us and how much he wants us to love each other. *Loving My Neighbour* takes us on a journey through the challenging terrain of how we can truly love one another, individually and in our communities. Daily Bible readings and reflections from Ash Wednesday to Easter Day explore how we can love in truth, love the vulnerable and the suffering, embrace difference, care for our world, and love ourselves as God loves us. Holy Week brings us back to reflect on Christ on the cross, who loved us to the very end.

Loving My Neighbour
A Lenten journey
Inderjit Bhogal, Joanna Collicutt, David Gregory, Esther Kuku, Sanjee Perera, Gemma Simmonds and John Swinton
edited by Olivia Warburton
978 1 80039 215 1 £9.99

brfonline.org.uk

BRF Ministries

Inspiring people of all ages to grow in Christian faith

BRF Ministries is the
home of Anna Chaplaincy,
Living Faith, Messy Church
and Parenting for Faith

As a charity, our work would not be possible without
fundraising and gifts in wills.
To find out more and to donate,
visit brf.org.uk/give or call +44 (0)1235 462305

Registered with
FUNDRAISING
REGULATOR